M

DATE DUE

MAY 6 - 2003	
JUL 8 - 2003	
JUN 14 2008	

DEMCO, INC. 38-2931

APR 0 2 2003

THE EXECUTION
OF A
SERIAL KILLER

ONE MAN'S EXPERIENCE
WITNESSING
THE
DEATH PENALTY

By
Joseph D. Diaz, Ph.D.

PONCHA PRESS
Morrison, Colorado

Editor: Pamela Eades
Cover photo: Joseph D. Diaz, Ph.D.
Cover photo adjustment: Joshua Oberloh
Graphic design consultant: Linda K. Murdock

ISBN: 0-9701862-7-4
Copyright © 2002
Joseph D. Diaz, Ph.D.

This is a true story. Except for that of the serial killer, Edward Castro, the names have been changed to ensure the privacy of those involved.

For information contact
Poncha Press
PO Box 280
Morrison, CO 80465
www.ponchapress.com
info@ponchapress.com

**Library of Congress Control Number:
2002113301**

Limited First Edition

Printed in the United States of America
10 9 8 7 6 5 4 3 2 1
First printing, 2002

THE **EXECUTION**

OF A

SERIAL KILLER

ONE MAN'S EXPERIENCE
WITNESSING
THE
DEATH PENALTY

ACKNOWLEDGEMENTS

There were many people who helped my in the crafting of this book. One of them was my friend and colleague, Dr. Cathy Cowan of Southwest State University, who paid for most of my trip to Florida and asked nothing in return. She passed away unexpectedly in December 2001, one year after the Castro execution. I miss her smiling face and gentle encouragement, and remember her often.

I am grateful to the Department of Sociology at the University of Nevada Las Vegas, and to Dr. Kriss Drass from the Department of Criminal Justice there. From them I received encouragement, a great education, and the confidence to engage in new and untried research approaches.

At Southwest State University in Marshall, Minnesota, my current academic home, every member of the Department of Social Sciences has offered me kind words and advice. They have enriched my life and I value my friendship with each one of them.

Extra thanks go to Bill Pavot who, along with Cathy, helped pay for the trip to Florida. Thanks also to Vicky Brockman and Eric Markusen, who both gave me encouragement, pep talks, and great advice. Thanks to my good friend and colleague Corey Butler, who read an early version of this manuscript and helped me to develop my thoughts further. I appreciate their support, and it was a pleasure to work with each of them.

There were others who assisted me along this foreign path. They include: the Florida State Prison at Starke, the National Coalition for the Abolition of the Death Penalty in Washington, D.C., CLUES in St. Paul, MN, Rick Robinson, Matt Scott, Onnie Diaz, Aaron Bitner, Russ

Tillett, Bob Parker, Donald Carns, David Dickens, Fred Preston, Simon Gottschalk, the music by the bands TOOL and Pink Floyd, and the writings of Will Christopher Baer, Stephen King, and Kurt Vonnegut. And finally, my thanks to the great students of Southwest State University and the community of Marshall, Minnesota.

But most of all, thanks go to my three little boys who keep reminding me that it is very important to tickle other people and to wrestle around on the living room floor whenever possible. And, of course, to my wife Camille, who begged me not to go to Florida that day, but who still held me through the horrible dreams and comforted me during the fear and uncertainty that followed what I witnessed.

INTRODUCTION

On Dec. 7, 2000, I sat less than three feet away from a serial killer named Edward Castro as the State of Florida executed the man. It was the first killing I had ever watched, and I quickly understood that the difference between killing and living is not always as clear as I had thought it to be.

Nearly six months after I took part in the execution of Edward Castro, or "my execution" as I've come to understand the event, the death penalty came to the forefront of our nation's collective consciousness. America, and indeed much of the world, focused its attention on the pending execution of Timothy McVeigh. Unlike most executions in the United States, scores of people would witness this man's death.

On June 11, 2001, McVeigh was scheduled to die for his part in the bombing of a federal office building in Oklahoma City, an act of violence that took the lives of 168 men, women, and children. Having witnessed an execution for myself, I followed the case with great personal and professional interest. On that June day, family members and others affected by McVeigh's crime literally lined up at the door to watch his death via closed-circuit television.

The morning before McVeigh's scheduled execution, I received a phone call from a producer for Canadian Public Radio, asking me if I was the same Dr. Joseph Diaz who had watched an execution recently. Surprised that they had heard of me, I told them that I was indeed that man. The station wanted to interview me on the air during McVeigh's execution the following day. There were, of course, no news cameras allowed inside of McVeigh's execution, and they wanted me to describe to their listeners what the inside of a death chamber looks like. They also wanted to know how a witness might feel during and after they observed the administration of our country's death penalty.

Over the six months that had passed since I witnessed my execution, I had given several television interviews on the subject of executions and the death penalty. I figured I might as well do another. Soon after I agreed to talk with them, my phone began ringing and by the end of the following day, June 11, 2001, I was exhausted from the nearly 20 and televison interviews I had given, which were broadcast all over the United States and Canada.

On June 12, the next morning, I woke up and thought to myself how relieved I was that June 11 was over; then, to my surprise, I began laughing out loud. My wife looked at me as if I were crazy and asked what was so funny. I replied, "Did you notice anything yesterday? June 11? Our wedding anniversary. Timothy McVeigh was executed on our anniversary and we both overlooked it." The remainder of that day, I turned off the television or radio anytime McVeigh's execution was mentioned. After missing my own anniversary because of an execution, I didn't want the death penalty interfering any further with my family.

The level of media interest in my story stunned me. The questions, regardless of the interviewer, news program, or media outlet, were generally the same. What is it like to witness an execution? How did it make you feel? Would you ever witness another execution? This book attempts to answer those questions. It is my hope that the reader will:

- Look into the mind of a serial killer and learn the genesis of his deadly urges;

- Gain an understanding of the experience of an execution; what one witness felt before, during, and in the horrible hours after he took part in the killing of another human being;

- Finally, and most importantly, ask him or herself, "Could *I* witness an execution? And if I did, how might *I* feel about it?"

— Joseph D. Diaz, Ph.D.

CHAPTER ONE

Edward Castro was a violent and dangerous man. At the age of 36, he was charming and physically strong. Castro lived from one day to the next with no direction or goal in his life, other than meeting his basic needs: food and alcohol. Much of his time and money was spent drinking in bars and he was, by that point, a chronic and severe alcoholic who would drink himself into a numb oblivion whenever possible. In the fall of 1986, his rage, which had been building for years, was about to tear itself out of his control.

As a drifter, Castro had developed the habit of hitchhiking from town to town, in search of whatever drove him onward. He made money both legally, as a repairman and performing odd jobs, and illegally, through theft, robbery, and fencing stolen property. When it wasn't possible to steal what he needed from a potential victim, he learned that he could acquire money through prostitution. Castro would offer himself sexually to other men in exchange for food, clothing or money. Although he often maintained that he was neither gay nor bisexual, he had countless homosexual encounters and would frequent gay bars while looking for victims, often robbing men that were attempting to pick him up for sexual encounters. Both men and women were attracted to Edward Castro, and he would use either gender to meet whatever need he might have at any particular time. While he was attractive and easy to talk with, his disarming smile hid a disturbed mind that fantasized about the most horrible and violent acts imaginable.

After his arrest for murder in January 1987, authorities discovered that Castro had something in common with Ted Bundy and Jeffrey Dahmer. Like these better-known serial killers, Edward Castro appeared to be both charming and dangerous at the same time. One of his favorite methods for acquiring quick money, or a vehicle, was to charm potential victims until they trusted the flirtatious, smiling man. He would then steal whatever he wanted from these people once they were relaxed, comfortable, and had dropped their guard.

Also like Bundy and Dahmer, Edward Castro, whose childhood was one of torture and victimization, had developed a lust for blood and death that had been growing stronger over the years. By that fall, his wanderlust had dropped him in central Florida. The exact reason for this is unclear, however police do know that he had a former step-daughter in the general area. Once in Florida, he quickly fell into his usual behavior of drunkenness, petty theft and pursuit of potential victims to rob.

On Oct. 28, 1986, Castro was running a gas-card scam in Euwella, Florida, a town about 60 miles north of St. Petersburg. He had stolen a gas charge card and was using the card to buy fuel and other items. Castro would then peddle these items to people he met off the street. Castro's gas-card scam wasn't violent, and might not have even been a felony, but it began a series of events that resulted in murder.

While he was undertaking his petty crime, Castro met Rick Allen, another small-time crook looking to make some quick money. Allen was impressed with Castro's gas card scheme and the two struck up a conversation on easy, and illegal, ways to make money. Allen and Castro hung out together that day, and at some point decided to go to a bar. They were looking for a potential victim to rob. When the two criminals went searching for their victim, Castro knew that the crime they were planning had the potential to be much more severe and much more violent than a simple robbery.

Although he was never charged with a violent offense before the fall of 1986, Castro claimed that several years before moving to Florida, he had attacked a man with a knife. One associate of Castro's told authorities that the would-be killer had been defending himself in a bar fight after being attacked with a lead pipe. He asserted that Castro had only stabbed the victim after he had suffered a severe head and scalp injury inflicted by the man. Other than that incident, and suspicions of several others, there are no verifiable cases where Castro attacked or attempted to kill another human being. But on Oct. 28, 1986, Edward Castro began a violent crime spree that would eventually lead to his own execution.

In the bar that day in Euwella, Florida, Allen and Castro met Jason Miller and struck up a conversation with him. In his arrest report, Castro stated that, "we met him at a bar and anyways, you know, he liked me right off and we got to talking. He wasn't no faggot, I don't think. No, he wasn't no faggot."

After talking for a while in the bar, Miller invited Castro and Allen to his mobile home in a trailer park outside of town. There the three men continued to drink. Castro recounted the following conversation that occurred between he and Miller that night: "Anyways, he liked me right off and he got to talking to me and I was on the street [meaning that Castro had no place to live] and shit like that and I didn't have no place to go and he told me 'hey look ... I'll tell you what. If you need a job, I'll get you a job.' He was gonna get me a job the next day starting at $7.00 an hour [which was more than twice the minimum wage at the time]. He said 'you can work with me. You can live right here [with me].' "

Miller offered Castro a job and a place to stay for free while he "got on his feet." Several minutes later, Castro and Allen, the accomplices, quietly began talking about how to rob Miller. In his confession to police months later, Castro said "Me and [Allen], you know, he got me off to the side and told me, I guess that's what started it, cause he told me ... we gonna take this guy out [kill him] ... I wanted a car and he said, 'You know what we'll do man? ... As big as you [Castro] are, you take him and I'll stab him with a screwdriver.' And I thought about it and I said 'Well fuck it, man, if that's what you want to do, let's do it.' You know, I wanted the car [Miller's van] and I didn't give a shit."

After Castro and Allen decided to kill the generous and unsuspecting man, the three continued to drink together. They soon ran out of beer and Miller and Castro went to the store together to purchase another 12-pack. After they returned to the trailer, Allen and Castro, the two conspirators, got into a fight about something minor, but because they were both drunk it quickly escalated into Castro grabbing Allen and throwing him to the floor. Castro, who was very strong, grabbed hold of Allen, began choking him, and said, for no apparent reason, "Hey man, don't fuck with me and don't fuck with my friends or I'll kill you."

Allen was terrified and immediately left the trailer, leaving Castro and Miller alone. Miller, who was the potential victim all along, was now alone with the man who would kill him before the night was over.

Upon his arrest, Castro couldn't remember what he and Allen had fought about, but he does recall that when he told Allen, "Don't fuck with my friends," he was only saying that to try to lure Miller into believing that Castro wouldn't hurt him.

Castro describes the scene after Allen left: "So, we were inside the house, me and the guy were by ourselves and I sat there and I was talking to him, you know. I've got a way of twisting things [around], you know, but like I was the one that intended the robbery to begin with ... I convinced him [Miller] that the other guy was the guy that he would look out for and I told him ... [Allen] 'was talking about stabbing you with a screwdriver' and it scared the fuck out of him."

It is likely that Castro told Miller about the screwdriver to test Miller's response to feeling physically threatened. Violent offenders often target victims they perceive as weak because they believe such victims will pose less of a threat to them during the attack. When an offender expects a potential victim to fight or strongly defend himself, they will generally seek out a more passive victim that will put up less resistance.

Unfortunately for Miller, he got scared and became passive, rather than becoming assertive and defensive. Months later, Castro claimed to police that this was his first murder. If that were true, he would probably have been nervous. Castro might not have attacked Miller if he felt uncomfortable with, or afraid of, his potential victim. However, Miller didn't become aggressive with Castro, and the decision was fatal.

Over the next hour, Miller became more and more nervous around Castro, but didn't ask him to leave his home, nor did he try to escape from the trailer himself. Miller eventually suggested that they both call it a night and go to sleep. He told Castro to use his bedroom, located in the back of the trailer, while he slept in the living room. Miller probably did this to avoid being trapped in his own bedroom in the back of the trailer. He most likely wanted easy access to the front door in the event he was attacked by the house guest that he now began to see as a threat.

Castro went to the back bedroom and left Miller alone in his living room. Before leaving him, Castro noticed that, at some point, Miller had gotten a kitchen knife and was keeping it close to him. Miller's last chance to escape from his horrible fate came as he was left alone lying on the living room floor, wondering about the stranger he had invited into his home. But he still didn't leave the mobile home.

After several minutes in the back bedroom, Castro quietly tried to creep into the living room to determine if Miller was asleep. He was planning to attack Miller and steal his van, but had not yet, according to his own account, decided to kill him. As he slowly and quietly entered the living room, he saw that Miller was awake and terrified, staring directly at him. Miller's chance to escape had passed.

Castro charged at him, and there was a brief struggle for Miller's knife, which Castro won. The knife, which Miller had planned to use for defense, was now in the hands of a volatile and dangerous killer.

Castro, having taken Miller's knife away, screamed, "Hey man, you got no business threatening me with a fucking knife." Miller, who was scared and confused, replied that he wasn't threatening Castro with it, but had it "because it just felt secure." Sarcastically, Castro pointed the knife at his intended victim and replied, "Well, you ain't so fucking secure now."

With a final burst of fear driving him, the terrified Miller ran for the front door and was halfway outside when Castro grabbed his legs and knocked him down. They struggled as Castro kept yelling at Miller to give up and get back inside the house. Miller fought hard and got further outside the house and into the yard when Castro grabbed him again with one hand and, with the other hand, showed Miller his own knife. Castro was afraid that, with both he and Miller struggling and fighting outside the home, a scream by Miller might alert someone to call for help. He told the horrified Miller, "Man, this game ain't no fun ... pick [an eye] your left or right, because you can scream if you want, but I will stab you in the eyeballs 15 times before the cops get here."

Miller, afraid to resist any further, was dragged back into the trailer and to the back bedroom. There, Castro used the knife to rip the bed sheet into strips and tie his victim up. Miller did not yet know that Castro intended to kill him. He might have thought that since he cooperated with his attacker and was now bound with the torn sheets, the worst was now over. He would learn in moments that the worst had not yet begun.

Castro left his victim tied-up in the bedroom and went back into the kitchen. Miller didn't know why Castro had left him alone in the back bedroom and undoubtedly spent the time alone listening to his attacker opening and closing drawers and cupboards in the kitchen. He probably wondered what the man was searching for and assumed that he was looking for valuable items to steal.

At this point, Castro could have taken whatever he wanted and left. With Miller restrained, he posed no threat to Castro and could not have prevented him from stealing everything. Castro later claimed that the murder was committed during the act of a robbery, but before even beginning the robbery, Castro had something else on his mind.

After searching the kitchen for several minutes, Castro found what he was looking for. In one of the drawers he discovered a large butcher's knife, with a blade nearly 10 inches long. He picked up the massive knife, sadistically admired the weapon he intended to use on the man who, hours before, had generously offered him his help. Castro left the kitchen, walked down the hall and back toward the bedroom that would in moments become a slaughterhouse.

When Castro walked into the bedroom Miller immediately saw the knife and began begging for his life. He pleaded with Castro, who stood in the middle of the room with the knife in his hand and a subtle smile on his face. Castro, who had spent the first decade of his life being raped, tortured, and abused beyond description by older men, stood listening to the cries and pleas of his victim. When he was a child, he made similar horrified and tortured pleas to his attackers and found, time after time, that his begging to be spared did no good. Twenty years later he stood listening to this man, an older man, beg and plead with him to free, not hurt, him.

Castro stood in the middle of the room staring at the incapacitated victim, who had become a symbolic object of his rage. He gripped the knife firmly in his hand, stepped toward him, raised the butcher knife over his head and slammed it into the terrified man's chest. He stabbed Miller over and over and over again until his victim's chest was a mass of blood and knife wounds.

Miller had offered Castro friendship, a job, a home and help getting back on his feet. What he got in return was a horrible and painful attack. His blood-covered body was left lying in his own bed.

Castro then calmly searched the entire house looking for money, jewelry, watches and anything else that he could sell for money. He left the house, taking Miller's van with him. He had no place to go, but had decided that he had stolen enough property to pay for his drinking binge for the immediate future.

The adrenaline rush of the violent murder he had just committed soon wore off, and Castro became frightened that the police would catch him. Determined to get away from the crime scene as quickly as possible, he fled to St. Petersburg, Florida. Without a place to live and driving a stolen van, he panicked and checked himself into an inpatient program for alcoholics, where he stayed for six days. He was afraid that being out on the road made him too conspicuous and much more likely to get caught, and the inpatient program offered him some security and anonymity while the police searched for the killer.

At the end of the six days in the rehab center, Castro was still afraid. He readmitted himself, but this time for 28 days. But when those four weeks had passed, Castro suspected that the police might still be actively working on the month-old murder case, and again checked himself into the clinic for an additional two weeks. Other than his early childhood years, Castro's time in the alcohol rehabilitation center in the fall of 1986 was one of the longest periods of sobriety in his life.

It is unclear whether Castro was simply trying to hide from the police in rehab or if the violent murder he had committed had scared him into trying to reform himself. But seven weeks after Jason Miller's murder, the killer was released from the inpatient center and spent Christmas with friends in St. Petersburg, Florida.

CHAPTER TWO

On Jan. 1, 1987, Edward Castro stole a small car, a Datsun, and drove the 25 miles from St. Petersburg to Tampa, Florida. Within two days he was arrested for public drunkenness and the developing serial killer found himself behind bars. By that point, the police in Euwella had found Miller's body, and the grisly murder scene, and were now searching for an unknown killer. If the Euwella police had known the name of the suspect, they could have issued an all points bulletin, or APB, for "Edward Castro." Such a move would have alerted the Tampa police, and the killer would never have been released from the jail cell to murder again. But the Euwella police had no name for their suspect, and could therefore issue no alerts to other police departments in the area. No one knew that Edward Castro, the man in the Tampa jail cell for public drunkenness, was a killer, and was anxious to find his next victim.

As a result, Castro was sentenced to 60 days of probation and released from police custody on Saturday, Jan. 3. After regaining his freedom, Castro took a bus back to St. Petersburg, arriving at 9:00 p.m. Having no money, he wasted little time seeking his next victim.

The day after his return to St. Petersburg, Castro found himself in a gay bar called The Club. He had been to the bar many times before, attracted to the $3.00 "all you can drink" policy, and the availability of potential victims. He intended to get drunk and look for someone to hustle. Castro knew that many homosexual men were not open about their sexuality. For fear of losing their jobs or their status in society, such men were less likely to file a police report about another man they met in a gay bar who had robbed them.

While Castro's intent was to rob a man, he also found that his lust for blood and death was growing stronger after the murder of Jason Miller. At around 2:00 a.m., a very drunk Castro was still drinking at the bar. He saw a well-dressed man walk into the bar alone. The killer approached the smiling man, who turned out to be Robert Edwards, a successful architect. Castro charmed and flirted with Edwards, until he was eventually invited back to the architect's home.

Castro later remarked that he thought that Edwards was either desperate for sex or was feeling dangerous because the two men were quite obviously ill-matched. Edwards was educated, wealthy, clean and refined, while Castro clearly looked like the rough, crude drifter that he was. After his arrest, Castro commented to police that Edwards brought him home thinking he was "going to make it," meaning have sex with Castro. But, Castro stated, while Edwards thought he was going to have sex, "[He] didn't know he was already dying."

Robert Edwards shared the rent on a beautiful, luxurious home with one roommate, a physician. Castro later stated that the gorgeous house, furnishings, and decor had impressed him. At the home, Castro and Edwards continued to flirt with each other playfully and soon went to Edwards' bedroom, where Castro maintained that he "blacked out," rather than admitting to willingly having sex with Edwards.

In his arrest report and confession, when describing his crimes to police, every time Castro's story reached the point of a homosexual encounter, he would claim that he blacked out, rather than admit his true sexuality. The fact that he easily admitted committing several violent murders, but would not admit to being gay, is both disturbing and fascinating. That tendency most likely stems from the guilt and shame he felt from being a victim of homosexual rape as a child, which is discussed later.

Rather than "blacking out," Castro most likely had sex with Edwards. He then asked if he could use the architect's shower to clean himself. Alone in the bathroom, Castro took what little money he had and hid it under a rug while he showered. He was still so intoxicated that when he finished showering, he couldn't remember where he had hidden his money. Thinking that the wealthy Edwards had stolen his small sum of money, he, in his own words, "just snapped."

Castro got dressed, exited the bathroom, and found Edwards in his bedroom. He began screaming at the man, demanding to know why Edwards had stolen his money. Edwards became scared and pointed to his dresser telling Castro that his (Edwards') wallet was in the top drawer and Castro could take all his money if he wished. Edwards believed that Castro, who was inebriated and screaming incoherently about money, was trying to rob him. Castro was not, at this point, trying to rob Edwards, but used the opportunity to steal his money anyway.

Castro snatched the man's wallet but continued his angry shouting. By this time, Edwards was scared and began to suspect he was now in real physical danger. Edwards held his hands up and asked Castro to try to relax and not to hurt him. The charming, flirtatious man that the architect had met in the bar only hours before, was gone. In his place stood a hardened killer, whose lust for death had been aroused.

Castro rushed at the frightened man and quickly overpowered him. Then, as he had done with Miller two months before, he tied-up the begging, pleading man. Edwards must have wondered when this man, who he had been intimate with just 20 minutes earlier, had decided to attack him. After securing his next victim to his own bed, Castro then left the incapacitated man in his room.

Perhaps as Miller might have done two months before, Edwards probably concluded that robbery was Castro's real motive for going home with him that night. As he lay alone in the bedroom, he must have wondered how he was going to free himself after his attacker left the house. Robert Edwards would never live to learn that it would be days before he would be found and untied, long after Castro was through with him that night.

The killer left Edwards alone on the bed and proceeded into the spacious kitchen to search for his favorite weapon, a large knife. Just as he had done in Miller's dirty, run-down trailer, he opened every drawer in the beautiful and modern kitchen searching for just the right instrument. With a razor-sharp butcher's knife in hand, Castro walked back toward the bedroom to fill his sadistic hunger for murder.

When the dangerous drifter reappeared in the bedroom, Edwards immediately saw the weapon and began thrashing around. Castro held the knife up, placing it menacingly on Edwards' face. He then very calmly said to the terrified man, "You've only got one life to live. Pick a spot." Castro had discovered he liked psychologically torturing his victims before ripping them apart, and was inviting Edwards to pick where the first stab wound from the heavy-bladed knife would penetrate him.

Edwards pleaded with the killer to spare his life, but Castro simply looked at the horrified man for a moment and then violently slammed the sharp butcher's knife into his trembling body. Edwards, whose hands were tied up over his head, screamed and gasped as his killer continued to stab him at least eight times in the chest. Castro concentrated his attack on the area near his victim's heart and the gaping knife wounds soon filled the man's lungs with blood. The last image that Robert Edwards, the successful and gentle architect, ever saw was the face of Edward Castro, his lover and murderer.

Before leaving the dead man's home, Castro took the money from his victim's wallet and whatever jewelry he could find. He scrawled anti-homosexual epithets on the walls and left Edwards' bloody corpse tied up and lying on the bed. The crime scene was not discovered for another two days, and by the time police had begun their investigation, Castro had again left the area, this time for Ocala, Florida.

CHAPTER THREE

Castro's tendency to drift from one town to another, seeking out new homosexual victims in different geographical areas, is eerily familiar to those of us who study the patterns of serial killers. Four years earlier, Larry Eyler, a serial murderer in the upper Midwest, demonstrated similar behavior. From October 1982 until August 1984, Eyler bound, strangled, and stabbed to death at least 21 gay men in Illinois, Indiana, Kentucky, and Wisconsin.

Unlike Castro, Larry Eyler was not a drifter, but had a home in Terre Haute, Indiana. He would leave his house and travel to neighboring states, searching for gay men to attack. To find his victims, Eyler typically "cruised" streets frequented by gay male prostitutes, or he picked up men in gay bars. He would then offer the men money to have sex with him.

Eyler would drive his victim outside of town, to a secluded area where the screams could not be heard, and tie him up under the pretense of having masochistic sex. However, after the sexual act, with his potential victim still restrained, as Castro's were, Eyler would then choke the man into submission. Eyler also often displayed a weapon, such as a knife, to the terrified men, describing what he was about to do to them. Sometimes he would gently caress his bound and struggling victim with the blade of the knife. He would tease the men, almost sexually, with soft statements like, "You know this is coming, don't you?" before stabbing them to death.

On a few occasions, Eyler would not kill his victims. He would pick up a man, tie and gag him, and proceed to have sex with the restrained man. But rather than kill him, Eyler would untie the stranger and let him live. One theory to explain such behavior is that some serial killers are driven by the desire to feel greater and greater levels of sexual stimulation. Their killings are a way to have a more extreme form of sex. However, at times, tying up a victim and having brutal sexual intercourse may be enough to satisfy the attacker. When murder is not "needed" for them to climax, it could be that the victim simply did not overly arouse the killer.

Castro, too, had exhibited such behavior. In the series of murders committed by Edward Castro, there is one known incidence where this killer decided to let the victim live, after first tying him up and teasing him with a knife. This particular attack occurred on the final day of Castro's murder spree.

The robbery that accompanied the vicious murder of architect Robert Edwards provided Castro with the money he needed to survive for the time being. However, it failed to satisfy another desire that was growing stronger in him by the day. He craved the sadistic gratification of attacking and killing other men. As had become his modus operandi, Castro sought to satisfy his blood lust at the same time that he satisfied his need for money and transportation.

It was Jan. 5, and two days had passed since the murder of Edwards. Castro wanted a new victim, but was afraid to visit any of the St. Petersburg gay bars. The killer feared that police would have a description of him from a witness who might have seen Castro leave The Club with Robert Edwards.

So instead of the gay bar, Castro went to a St. Petersburg grocery store. At the supermarket, he soon met another man in the parking lot and asked him for a ride to

Ocala, in exchange for money. This next potential victim agreed and the two men set off together for the two hour drive to Ocala, Florida.

During the drive, Castro tried to appear charming and calm to ease the nerves of the unknown driver. His plan was to allow the driver to reach Ocala, where he would direct him to a quiet or remote area. There, Castro intended to choke the man into submission, with his bare hands, and then stab him to death with a small knife he carried with him.

When the trip ended in Ocala, Castro decided against attacking the intended victim, for reasons unknown even to the murderer himself. The driver stopped at the address Castro had given him and the killer simply smiled, shook his hand and got out of the car. The driver never suspected, and probably doesn't to this day, that his unknown passenger was a violent serial killer who had targeted him as his next victim. Because of a simple mood change by Castro, this man's life was spared. But Ocala, Florida would still be the scene of Castro's final, and most violent, murder.

To put it bluntly, Edward Castro had become a serial killer and he thrived on it. His crimes provided him with money and served as an outlet for his violent and sexual urges. He loved the rush he felt when violating and destroying older gay men. His behavior had begun something of a chain reaction in him. Unless stopped, it would continue to escalate until he felt the constant need to kill. Ocala would be the city where Castro's haunting and controlling personality would reach its most horrible pinnacle.

―――――――――

Castro believed that the police were looking for him and he was, in his words, "hiding out." He stayed briefly at the home of the daughter of his former wife, before he met Aaron Hernando, the maintenance man of an Ocala apartment complex. Castro and Hernando, also an alcoholic, drank together on a couple of occasions.

On Jan. 14, 1988, while staying at Hernando's apartment, Castro met another drifter, Richard Williams. Williams, a 17-year-old from Iowa, was hitchhiking from Florida back home to the Midwest. How the two met, and the nature of their relationship at the time, is unclear. But at some point during that first day of their acquaintance, Castro decided that the young man would be his next victim.

His decision to kill Williams marked a turning point in the behavior of this serial killer. For the first time his victim had no home and was younger than Castro. It is likely, that Castro's escalating, violent sexual urges led him to no longer target a specific type of person. Instead, he was now preying on anyone he encountered.

Castro had a key to Hernando's apartment, where, on that January day, he and Williams drank beer together. After about an hour, they moved onto Hernando's bed, where Castro immediately attacked the quiet young man.

Ocala, in exchange for money. This next potential victim agreed and the two men set off together for the two hour drive to Ocala, Florida.

During the drive, Castro tried to appear charming and calm to ease the nerves of the unknown driver. His plan was to allow the driver to reach Ocala, where he would direct him to a quiet or remote area. There, Castro intended to choke the man into submission, with his bare hands, and then stab him to death with a small knife he carried with him.

When the trip ended in Ocala, Castro decided against attacking the intended victim, for reasons unknown even to the murderer himself. The driver stopped at the address Castro had given him and the killer simply smiled, shook his hand and got out of the car. The driver never suspected, and probably doesn't to this day, that his unknown passenger was a violent serial killer who had targeted him as his next victim. Because of a simple mood change by Castro, this man's life was spared. But Ocala, Florida would still be the scene of Castro's final, and most violent, murder.

To put it bluntly, Edward Castro had become a serial killer and he thrived on it. His crimes provided him with money and served as an outlet for his violent and sexual urges. He loved the rush he felt when violating and destroying older gay men. His behavior had begun something of a chain reaction in him. Unless stopped, it would continue to escalate until he felt the constant need to kill. Ocala would be the city where Castro's haunting and controlling personality would reach its most horrible pinnacle.

Castro believed that the police were looking for him and he was, in his words, "hiding out." He stayed briefly at the home of the daughter of his former wife, before he met Aaron Hernando, the maintenance man of an Ocala apartment complex. Castro and Hernando, also an alcoholic, drank together on a couple of occasions.

On Jan. 14, 1988, while staying at Hernando's apartment, Castro met another drifter, Richard Williams. Williams, a 17-year-old from Iowa, was hitchhiking from Florida back home to the Midwest. How the two met, and the nature of their relationship at the time, is unclear. But at some point during that first day of their acquaintance, Castro decided that the young man would be his next victim.

His decision to kill Williams marked a turning point in the behavior of this serial killer. For the first time his victim had no home and was younger than Castro. It is likely, that Castro's escalating, violent sexual urges led him to no longer target a specific type of person. Instead, he was now preying on anyone he encountered.

Castro had a key to Hernando's apartment, where, on that January day, he and Williams drank beer together. After about an hour, they moved onto Hernando's bed, where Castro immediately attacked the quiet young man.

CHAPTER FOUR

Several years had passed between Edward Castro's first known knife attack in El Cajon, California, where he was defending himself in the bar fight, and the murder of Jason Miller in Euwella, Florida, though authorities strongly suspect he committed many other murders in between those two events. The length of time between Castro's first and second known attacks is not unusual for serial killers. Jeffery Dahmer, who murdered and ate 15 young boys, killed his first man after having sex with him in 1978. He then did not kill again until nine years later, in 1987. But once he resumed the killing, Dahmer regularly murdered young men until his arrest in July 1991. The multi-year lapse in killing certainly occurs in serial murder, and it generally happens, as it did with both Castro and Dahmer, between the first and second victims.

But Castro's violent desires were clearly escalating and consuming him more and more. The time between the killing of Jason Miller and that of Robert Edwards was approximately two months. Yet less than 24 hours had passed since Edwards' murder when Castro planned to kill the stranger who gave him a ride to Ocala.

The initial shock of violently murdering an innocent person quickly passed for Castro. He could get money, sex, cars, and anything else he desired without worrying that a robbery or assault victim might give his description to the police. He soon realized that he enjoyed killing and that murder served his needs, both visceral and financial, very well.

killed the police officers and continued to run. Instead, he was brought in for questioning. Again, he confessed to the three killings, this time to detectives.

Interestingly, Castro told the police, while still standing in the gas station parking lot, that Williams was innocent of everything and knew nothing of the killings. Unsure if the man confessing had actually killed anyone, the police released his young companion. Later, after police realized that multiple killings had taken place, they arrested Richard Williams at the local bus station. He was brought in for further questioning about the murders only after Castro told detectives that back in Ocala he had forced the young man to stab the corpse of Steven Carter.

Several detectives conducted the initial interview with Edward Castro. During this time, he was pleasant, respectful and cordial to each of them. He truly enjoyed talking about what he had done, and told them that it felt good to "get it off my chest." Castro also showed a sense of loyalty to his arresting officers. He told detectives several times that he wanted the patrol officers who stumbled across him at the gas station to get credit for "bringing him in." This behavior and Castro's insistence that Richard Williams was innocent, reveals another side of the serial killer: one that almost appears human in the sense of loyalty to others.

At no time during the interview did Castro ask for a lawyer, even though the officers had read him the Miranda rights and he knew that a lawyer was available to him. At several points during his initial interview with detectives, Castro commented that he knew he was going to spend "the rest of my life in jail." Castro was at times incoherent, however, and did ask for a psychiatrist.

After his confession was signed and his statement made, the exhausted Castro was taken to a jail cell, where he would wait for police to take the next step. As the metal door was closing behind him, locking the killer into his cell, a frightening thought occurred to Castro. He cleared his throat and asked the jailer, "Uh ... hey, does Florida have the death penalty?"

Had Castro requested a lawyer during his confession, instead of a psychiatrist, his counsel would have informed him of Florida's death penalty. With the knowledge of execution as a possible punishment for his crimes in Florida, Castro might not have been so open about his actions. But during the interview, it never occurred to Castro that he might be executed for his crimes.

The jailer finished locking the cell and replied to Edward Castro, "Yes, sir, it does." He then walked away, leaving the serial killer alone, sitting on the cot in his small cell. For the first time, it occurred to Castro that the death penalty might be used to end his horrible life.

Twelve years later, a young professor looked into the face of Edward Castro as the State of Florida administered that penalty.

CHAPTER FIVE

I was not thinking about murderers and executions during the hot and humid summer of 2000. Instead, my focus was on the summer school course I taught at Southwest State University in Marshall, Minnesota, where I had been a Professor of Sociology and Criminology for only nine months. Prior to that time I had taught various classes at the Department of Sociology at the University of Nevada Las Vegas (UNLV), and at UNLV's Department of Criminal Justice. Southwest State University was my first permanent, full-time academic appointment.

Upon completion of my Ph.D., I found that my student loans had become due. During college, the loans had saved my credit rating and helped me avoid writing bad checks to pay for groceries. Ten years of college and two advanced degrees had resulted in a student loan debt that was equal to the cost several new cars put together plus a down-payment on a small home. To help dig out of debt, I agreed to teach Introduction to Sociology as a summer school class that year, a job that paid $3,000 for about one month of work.

My typical day that summer month started around 7 a.m., when I arose and watered my struggling and terminally-ill vegetable garden. I would then feed my struggling and terminally-grumpy children, and make the three-minute drive to the university. For three hours, four times each week, I lectured to students who were apparently even less excited about summer school than I was. Consequently, few students ever waited after classes to ask me questions or seek further explanation of the day's discussion. This allowed me to go straight home after class, bypassing my boiling-hot office on campus.

About halfway through the four-week course, one student asked if he could talk to me in my office after class. He told me that the topic was serious, and he would appreciate it if we could talk privately in my office. I agreed to meet with him and arrived at my office before he did. While waiting to help with this young man's crisis, whatever it was, I checked the news on the Internet. I wanted to see if anyone famous had died or if presidential candidate George W. Bush had said anything unintentionally funny the day before.

I noticed a news story that immediately piqued my interest. The headline on the ABC News Internet page read, "States Struggle to Find Execution Witnesses." As a researcher with an interest in crime and violent destructive behavior, I read the story immediately. I learned that several states were having difficulty finding individuals willing to serve as official witnesses during the executions of prisoners.

Two states in particular, Florida and Texas, the states with the highest number of executions each year, were hard-pressed to find willing spectators for their executions. The shortage of witnesses in those two areas struck me as odd since I understood that most citizens of Florida and Texas were proponents of the death-penalty. I remembered reading an article in the *Houston Chronicle* a couple of years earlier in which a journalist reported that recent research had found 61 percent of people in the state of Texas were in favor of the death penalty. It seemed reasonable to me that if an individual supported the death penalty, he should be willing to watch an execution take place. Indeed, I would discover months later that although most people in these two states might be in favor of executions, almost no one wants to actually watch one in person.

At this time, the summer of 2000, I did not favor the use of the death penalty, nor did I strongly oppose it. My indecision was not from lack of thought about the issue. In fact, as a professor studying and teaching about crime, violence, homicide and society's response to these social ills, I had thought about and talked about the death penalty a great deal. But at that point, I had not yet made up my mind whether or not the death penalty was morally right. Frankly, I wasn't sure it was even a moral issue at all.

An incident involving a family friend in my home state of Illinois further confused the issue for me. There, a young man sat on death row for the rape and murder of a young girl. The accused man's father had worked with one of my family members for quite some time, and through that relationship the inmate had become known to my family. The young man maintained his innocence throughout the entire time he waited on death row. Eventually DNA tests on the semen found in the murdered child proved that he did not commit the crime and the wrongly-convicted man was exonerated. But being on death row, he had nearly lost his life for a crime he did not commit.

Since 1977, 13 other cases like this have also occurred in Illinois. This led Governor George Ryan to halt, indefinitely, all executions in Illinois on Jan. 31, 2000, until the state could investigate the fairness and relevancy of its death penalty. In his statement, the Republican Governor said, "I cannot support a system, which in its administration, has proven so fraught with error, and has come so close to the ultimate nightmare: the State's taking of innocent life."

Mirroring Governor Ryan's decision in Illinois was a similar action in Maryland by Governor Parris Glendening. In that state, only 28 percent of the population is African

American, yet 80 percent of Maryland's death row inmates are black. Additionally, of the African Americans on death row in Maryland, 90 percent of them were sentenced to death for murders committed against Caucasians. In effect, African Americans are being executed in Maryland at over three times their rate of the population in the state, and almost every inmate on death row is there for killing a Caucasian.

On May 9, 2002, Governor Glendening placed a moratorium on all executions in Maryland until the issue of racism in the application of the death penalty could be researched. While Governor Glendening's reasons for halting all executions in Maryland differed from those cited by Governor Ryan of Illinois, the two governors observed the same issue: The death penalty is not administered fairly.

However, for me the issue was still not always clear, despite the sad case of our family friend, the problems with the death penalty in my home state of Illinois, and the numerous scientific studies arguing that the death penalty does not decrease the rate of violent crime. I had still not yet taken a definitive position on this form of punishment in our society. Just about every time academic reason began to sway me toward opposing the death penalty, I would open the newspaper and read a story about a killer who just did not seem worthy of life.

Over the previous year, one case in particular had been weighing heavily on my mind, causing me to sway toward supporting the death penalty in certain extreme cases. My wife and I, and our young children, were living in Las Vegas while I worked on my doctorate in sociology. As I wrote my dissertation, during the summer of 1999, I sold cellular phones part-time at a booth inside a local grocery store. There must have been a hundred grocery stores in Las Vegas, but the one where I worked was in located in a busy section of west Las Vegas.

As I set up the booth for a day of sales and studying for school, an employee of the store approached me, and wanted to know if I had heard about what happened earlier that morning. He told me that some guy walked into the grocery store, next door to the very one I worked in, and began randomly killing people with a shotgun. This took place as I started my day that morning, shaving, showering, and thinking about what part of my dissertation I was going to work on.

I learned the full story over the following weeks and, along with everyone else in Las Vegas, was sickened by the brutality of the event. Several hours before the grocery store shooting began that hot summer morning, the killer had already started his crime spree. A 23-year-old man named Zane Floyd summoned a private dancer to the house he shared with his parents in west Las Vegas. When the girl arrived, he tied her up and repeatedly raped her. Finished with her, Floyd then told his victim he was going out to kill the first 19 people as he could find and left the dancer restrained in the house. Dressed in combat fatigues and carrying a 12-gauge shotgun under his coat, he walked to the grocery store closest to his home.

As Zane Floyd approached the supermarket, he sighted his first victim, a male employee at the store's entrance, lining up the carts for the day of shoppers. The unknowing man was facing away from the killer, who raised the barrel of the shotgun and blew the victim's head apart. Next Floyd jogged into the grocery store, nearly empty in the early morning hours, shooting as many people as he could find. By the time police arrived, he had killed four people and critically injured several others.

The angry brutality and senselessness of the crimes, as well as their geographical proximity to my family, shocked and horrified me. News cameras showed Floyd after his arrest, in the back of a police car, smiling and laughing about what he had done. I thought to myself, "this man simply not deserve to live."

Over the next two years, additional information emerged about Floyd. At the time of his arrest, he had told authorities that he had always wanted to kill someone. He thought it would be fun to do and would provide him with a great feeling of power. Zane Floyd said his dream was to fight in a war, so he could murder as many people as he wanted. His trip through the grocery store that morning fulfilled a fantasy he had been dreaming about for years.

In my shocked and enraged mind, this killer had gone so far beyond the norms of acceptable human behavior that we as a society could not pretend that he was one of us any more. On the day of the attack, I thought Zane Floyd, the cold-blooded and remorseless killer, who laughed at what he had done, was a worthy candidate for execution.

Yet, as a social scientist, I had studied the death penalty from many perspectives. Some argued in favor of capital punishment and some against it, and I considered each of these perspectives. My thinking tended to be influenced by the many studies that showed capital punishment was neither appropriate nor useful as a means of reducing crime rates in American society. But, while the studies were scientific and well-researched, they were strictly theoretical and unemotional. Whenever people like Zane Floyd decided that they were ready to show their inhumane desires to the world, my gut, my emotions, shifted back again to supporting the death penalty.

That summer day in 2000, when I read the news article in my office about witnesses and executions, I decided to look more closely at the death penalty than I had previously. Without much thought about the ramifications of my request, I sent a letter to the State of Texas and one to the State of Florida volunteering to serve as a witness at an execution. I hoped that by encountering an execution up close and interviewing people involved with the process, I could better understand the death penalty and come to a conclusion about my support for, or opposition to, the process. One year after Zane Floyd's crimes, which had occurred so close to my family and home, I still remained indecisive regarding the death penalty.

The short letter that I sent to Florida read:

July 21, 2000

To the Department of Corrections:

I am writing this letter to request being present during an execution of a prisoner by the State of Florida. I am neither opposed to, nor supportive of the death penalty, so my request has no political or ideological basis. I request this opportunity because, as a Professor of Sociology and Criminology, I often discuss the death penalty from the perspective of criminological theory, and I think that witnessing an execution will make me a more informed professional. I would like to stress, again, that I am not opposed to the death penalty and am in no way intending to use this experience to criticize the state of Florida and its criminal justice system. I simply believe that citizens have the responsibility to be present during executions. Further, as a criminologist and sociologist, I will be more informed on the subject of the death penalty, having witnessed its occurrence.

Thank you for your consideration in this matter. My curriculum vitae is enclosed, so please feel free to contact me at my provided phone number or address if you have any questions.

Sincerely,

Joseph D. Diaz, B.A., M.A., Ph.D.
Professor of Sociology & Criminology

As an undergraduate student, I once tried to telephone Queen Elizabeth from my dorm room in Arizona. While I did not expect to be connected, I tried anyway. Had I actually been connected to Her Royal Highness, I'm not sure what I would have said or if I would actually want to talk to her. But I thought it would be interesting to try.

When I sent the letters to Florida and Texas, I did not expect them to take me up on my offer to be present during an execution. With the luxury of believing the possibility was non-existent, I imagined what I would do if I was asked to serve. I imagined that I would willingly accept the opportunity and that, as a social scientist, I would find the experience informative and profoundly fascinating.

Later that day, after sending the two letters, I told my wife what I had done. Camille, who is a kind and gentle Christian woman, quickly looked my way to see if I was kidding her. She was disappointed to see that I was not. We peacefully yelled at each other for several minutes until I, ever the diplomat, pointed out that we were arguing needlessly. I would never be asked to witness an execution and the argument was, therefore, pointless.

Quickly supporting that thought, the Great State of Texas replied to my letter. The correspondence informed me that I did not meet their qualifications for watching an execution, since I was not a resident of the State of Texas. According to Texas State laws, I could not serve as an official witness for the State.

Unlike Texas, Florida did not immediately respond to my request. However, given the terse response by the government of Texas, I assumed Florida had better things to do than take the time to deny my request. Over the next several months, I continued my research into social problems of cultural minorities in the area and taught my courses at the university. I completely forgot my letter of request to witness the execution of a convicted death row inmate by the State of Florida.

CHAPTER SIX

Growing up as a young boy, my first thoughts about violence and death began when my dad introduced me to hunting, and I watched the death of animals. I was never comfortable with the idea of killing something else, or even taking part in such an activity; but, hunting with my father always held a fascination for me.

My parents divorced when I was a child. Although my dad made the effort to stay close to me, I grew up feeling that I didn't know him very well. I realized early on that he and I were unlike in most ways. I hated that my skin color was a light complexion like my mom's, rather than dark brown like my dad's, who came from Mexico and is of Aztec decent. Also, I wanted very badly to impress my father.

When I was around nine, my dad took me hunting for the first time. The two of us went hunting rabbit and pheasant one warm winter day in rural Illinois, accompanied by several of Dad's adult friends. I had never seen a gun before, but being an American kid with a television, I knew about guns and was fascinated and awe-struck by them. And that day, for the first time, I saw my dad carrying a gun. Dad's gun, to me, symbolized my father: strong, sleek, mysterious, inviting, and wonderfully unknown. I wanted to be close to it—and to him.

This man who I adored and admired, but didn't really know, was carrying a gun and smiling at me. I believed that I was the most important person in the world. I imagined that while Dad and I were together, with his big 12-gauge shotgun, we were the coolest people that had ever lived. I didn't get to carry the gun, but I found that it was enough for me just to be near my dad as he carried that much frightening power. I daydreamed that my dad's friends must have been talking among themselves, making comments like, "Boy, that Diaz kid seems really cool … just like a grown-up. He is standing right there next to his dad and that big gun, and he is not even afraid. He must be really special, and his dad must think he is the greatest kid in the world."

As we loaded up the truck to return home, Dad to his and me to mine, I wanted so badly to ask him if I could shoot his gun. I tried staring at the gun, willing him to notice my desire. But he didn't. I even tried touching the gun as it rested in the case. But that, too, failed to produce an invitation from Dad to shoot it.

On the drive home, I tried over and over again to work up the nerve to ask if I could shoot the gun. My dad's friends were in the truck with us and I didn't want them to know that I had never held a firearm before. I was afraid they might laugh at me or think I was a stupid little kid if my dad told me, "No, son, you're too young."

At some point my curiosity overcame my fear. I blurted out, "I wanted to shoot the gun today." My dad, who always tried to make every one of the short moments we spent together perfect for me, replied, "Oh, you should have told me. You could have shot it." My disappointment was obvious. Dad comforted me by saying that if I had fun that day, we could go out hunting again together. He even said that someday I could have my own gun.

We didn't kill anything that day. Still, I knew that I just done something significant. I had gone hunting for the first time, something that my dad enjoyed doing. In my innocent, 9-year-old mind, I believed that I would be a hunter for the rest of my life. I imagined my dad, this mysterious and intriguing man, with me every day on father and son hunting trips. Two years later, my mom, my brothers, and I moved from Illinois to Arizona and I never again hunted with my dad.

But I was determined to continue hunting to maintain that bond with my father. Throughout my junior high and high school years in Flagstaff, Arizona, I hunted animals with great fervor, though their death always bothered me. Over the years, I hunted white-tailed deer, mule deer, black bear, elk, antelope, wild turkey and many species of small game. I used this passion to screen prospective stepfathers my mom introduced to me. I peppered the unsuspecting men with questions about guns, attempting to weed out the unacceptable candidates.

But my favorite part of the hunt was calling my dad on the phone afterward. I would recount the events of the day, with a few embellishments to make myself sound more impressive. But I didn't tell Dad the whole story. I never confessed to him that I was always sickened at the sight of the dead animal. I could never "dress" the carcass, which involved cutting out the warm internal organs with a knife. I couldn't tell him that. Hunting seemed to have become the only thing that Dad and I had in common, and I didn't want to taint it.

By the time I turned 24, I had stopped hunting. I sold the last of my guns when my wife gave birth to our first child. I didn't particularly want to part with the sole remaining link between my father and I, but I feared that my child might be hurt accidentally if we kept a gun in the house. As hunting became less important in my life, and I realized that killing animals bothered me, I noticed that my dad and I had drifted further and further apart.

Early in the fall of 2000, I found myself thinking about my dad and decided to give him a call. As with all our phone conversations over the last few years, I couldn't draw him into a discussion. Most of the time, after several awkward minutes, one of us would become frustrated and find a reason to end the phone call, without ever saying anything of substance to one another.

On that particular day, however, we stumbled onto the subject of hunting. Dad was planning a deer-hunting trip in a few months and I found myself telling him that I missed the sport. Much to my surprise, as I thought about hunting that day, I did truly miss it.

Looking back on the phone call, I now know hunting was not what I missed. I missed my dad and the perfect adoration that we seemed to have for each other during my childhood years. That one hunting trip we had taken 20 years earlier still served as a bond between a father and a son who, otherwise, didn't know each other at all.

Within a week or two we talked on the phone again. Once more, the subject of our chat soon turned to hunting. I asked Dad if he wanted to come out to Minnesota, where I was now living, and go goose hunting in a few weeks. To my surprise, he agreed. I was happy my dad was coming to visit me, but I hadn't killed an animal in nearly a decade. During that time I had grown to consider the practice wrong for me. It did not seem right to find any kind of joy in the death of living creature. I had decided years before that I had been hunting for the wrong reasons and had stopped.

Yet several days later, I was cleaning a shotgun that I had borrowed from a friend in preparation for the upcoming hunt. My wife gently reminded me that I now thought killing animals for fun was wrong. I knew that Camille had a very good point, but I was afraid to listen to her further. I countered with the argument that my dad and I had not been close in years, and that this might help us grow together again. I avoided the real point of her statement because I knew that it was irrefutable. Camille knew that I was planning to do something that I did not believe was right and that, somehow, I expected to feel good about it afterward.

Shortly before goose season began, Dad called me from Illinois to tell me he would not come for another month or so. I was disappointed and angry. But I still had hope that the wait would be worth it. Eventually, he and I would be together again, talking, smiling, and simply enjoying each other's company.

On the first Saturday of goose season, I went out hunting by myself, probably thinking it would impress Dad, but I didn't shoot a single bird. I came home with my borrowed shotgun, my sparkling-new, blaze-orange clothing, and no goose. This scene occurred several times over the next week, until one Friday afternoon when I took my 3-year-old son, Nathaniel, with me.

I had never taken one of my sons hunting before and my wife was not pleased that I had invited Nathaniel to go along. But seeing how excited I became about my own dad when I talked about our past hunting trips, Camille agreed to allow our son to go. She probably never expected us to actually kill a goose, and therefore was not strongly opposed to the outing.

It was a cold and windy fall afternoon as Nathaniel and I set out in our rugged hunting vehicle: a new and spotless, green Nissan family-van, fully equipped with a TV and VCR. I drove toward a spot where I had seen geese several days before, near a small, stagnant lake. It was about a 25-minute drive from our house, and my young companion and I listened to Sesame Street tapes on the stereo and sang silly kids' songs. We were enjoying the time together.

I parked the van off the side of a dirt road, and Nathaniel and I began walking down a grass-covered footpath. Before we even reached the lake, we saw a goose take off, out from some reeds, and fly right over our heads.

I threw the shotgun to my shoulder and squeezed off a round, but missed the fast, enormous bird. I re-aimed and shot again a split-second later, hitting the target. The bird, now wounded, flew to the ground about 35 yards away from us. I put two more shells into my borrowed gun and, with my little child behind me covering his ears from the blast, quietly walked toward the place where the bird had gone down. After two or three minutes had passed, I saw the bird standing up on the ground, looking at me from about seven yards away.

My heart beating quickly, I smoothly raised my gun and shot the bird again in one fluid movement. I aimed for its head, so as not to destroy the meat. From that short distance, I watched as the poor thing exploded into a mess of blood, feathers and dirt from the surrounding ground.

My 3-year-old son walked with me over to the area where the poor, lifeless body lay on the ground. Only moments before, the bird had gracefully sailed over our heads, with a powerful and sleek majesty. But I, in a moment of insecure greed, had just destroyed the animal, reducing it to a crumpled, broken corpse.

Nathaniel jumped around with excitement, barely controlling himself. I, on the other hand, stood there feeling my self-respect quickly slipping away.

"Is it dead, Daddy? Did we kill it? Daddy, did you kill the bird? Your gun is LOUD, Daddy! Is that goose dead, Daddy? Can I hug the bird, Daddy? Look at its blood, oh yuck! How come birds have blood, too? Can I hold the bird? Is it dead, Daddy?"

Sickened, I could only reply, "Yes, son, I killed it. I killed that bird."

We drove home with the broken , bloody thing lying on the passenger-side floor of the van. For the entire trip, I fielded questions about why I had killed the bird. I tried to make my young son understand that I now thought what I had done was wrong, and that Daddy doesn't like to kill things.

When we got home, my wife and 5-year-old son came out of the house to meet us. Nathaniel immediately announced with great excitement, "We killed a goose! Daddy shot it with the gun and it had blood!" My wife gave me a soft, loving smile that I didn't quite understand. She asked if I was OK, even though she already knew that I wasn't.

I was nauseous as I laid the lifeless goose on the workbench in my garage and noticed that my wife was staring at me without saying anything. She sent the kids into the house and asked again, "Are you all right?"

"No," I answered flatly. "I don't think I should have done that. I don't think there is anything good that came out of me killing this bird and I feel just sick inside."

She turned and walked inside the house. The smell coming off the dead bird made me gag and I stifled the urge to vomit all over the blood-splattered floor. I stood alone in my garage, with bloody hands, crying to myself.

I wrapped the remains of the bird in a brown paper bag and gently placed it into our outside garbage can behind the garage. I removed the hunting license from my wallet and tore it up into tiny pieces, throwing it into the garbage next to the pitiful body of the goose. Earlier that day, I had so desperately wanted to kill the bird, and now a painful wave of nausea rolled over me. I closed my eyes and breathed through my nose to avoid vomiting into the garbage can and further desecrating the already-violated bird.

The physical sickness passed and I slowly walked back into the garage. I stripped off my hunting gear, which was splattered with tiny spots of blood, and went inside the house to be with my family. I spent most of the remaining afternoon talking to my confused boys and trying to explain how daddies sometimes make mistakes, too.

Ironically, I have never liked killing animals at all. I try to shoe bugs outside of the house rather than kill them. Once, while driving with my family, I almost crashed the car trying to avoid a mouse on the road. I even get slightly angry watching nature documentaries, when the predator lion captures and kills some unsuspecting antelope. I always root for the prey, and try to will the predator to become a vegetarian.

Despite all this, I somehow imagined that I could kill an animal myself, and that it wouldn't affect me adversely. I was wrong. That day I killed the goose, I felt a level of guilt and remorse that I had never before experienced. I knew that I could never, and would never, again willfully kill another living creature. I knew that I didn't have the right to take the life of something else simply for my pleasure. While I would not become a vegetarian, I would never again kill for sport or to satisfy my own insecurity. I realized that day that life, in all its countless forms, deserves to live.

On that late-summer afternoon, I decided that I would never again kill anything.

CHAPTER SEVEN

In the fall semester of 2000, I taught undergraduate students in an advanced Criminology course. The course explored the subject of crime, why it occurs and how we as a society respond to it. To address this difficult question, we studied many types of crimes and many types of offenders.

Our discussions attempted to answer many questions: Why would a sociopathic killer engage in cannibalism? Why do serial killers often have a history of bedwetting? What is the relationship between rape and aggression in offenders? Is the death penalty an effective deterrent to crime?

I remember one answer to that final question, given by one of my professors in graduate school. One day, in a class he was teaching, Professor Fred Preston remarked, "Of course the death penalty prevents crime. It must, because of all the killers who have been executed, none of them have gone on to commit additional crimes." Although this justification for the death penalty seemed weak to me, it's hard to argue with the rationale. When I expressed this perspective to my Criminology class one day, it definitely had its adherents among the group of students.

When I was a student, I disliked the style of some professors who would stand in the front of a class and lecture endlessly, without giving the students an opportunity to state their opinions about the subject. So, during each semester, I liked to hold "discussion days." On these designated sessions, the class would debate some relevant topic. As the professor, my role was to point out any flaws in the arguments made, in an effort to stimulate intelligent discussion. Previously, the group discussed topics such as: "When is it appropriate for courts to charge children as adults?" and "Is crime inherent to society?" During this particular class, we tackled the death penalty. The question I posed to the class was, "Should the death penalty continue? Why or why not?"

We hit all of the major arguments commonly used in support of the death penalty, exploring each one in turn. First, we tackled the idea that execution is the only way to make sure that killers don't wind up back on the street to kill again. But I had a hard time accepting the notion that humans could not develop a way to keep prisoners out of society without killing them.

In fact, I argued that an effective method for keeping violent offenders off the street has been utilized for at least 2000 years; the jail. To make sure that bad guys don't kill us anymore, we put them in a cell, lock the door, and then refuse to let them out, even when they ask very nicely. The bad guys will find it impossible to kill us, the good guys, if they can't ever leave their prison cell. "For this reason," I told my class that day, "we don't need to execute people to make sure that they don't kill others. We simply never let them out of prison."

"But there aren't enough prisons to hold all the criminals who deserve to be in one," countered a young woman from the third row.

"Then we need to be a little more careful about who we vote for," I responded. Although the prison system is a complex issue, I took the simplistic position that if there were not enough prisons for all the bad guys who kill people, we should vote for the politician that promises to build more of them. The candidate that tells the people, "I will make more prisons to make sure that bad guys don't get out and kill more people" should win the election.

resin, wax and sulfur melted together and then his body drawn and quartered by four horses and his limbs and body consumed by fire, reduced to ashes and his ashes thrown to the winds..."

After the punishment was announced, it was carried out and one observer of the execution described the horrible spectacle in the following way:

The sulfur was lit, but the flame was so poor that only the top skin of the hand was burnt, and that only slightly. Then the executioner, his sleeves rolled up, took the steel pincers, which had been especially made for the occasion, and which were about a foot and a half long, and pulled first at the calf of the right leg, then at the thigh, and from there at the two fleshy parts of the right arm; then at the breasts. Though a strong, sturdy fellow, this executioner found it so difficult to tear away the pieces of flesh that he set about the same spot two or three times, twisting the pincers as he did so, and what he took away formed at each part a wound about the size of a six-pound crown piece [a coin].

After these tearings with the pincers, Damiens [the man being tortured to death], who cried out profusely, though without swearing, raised his head and looked at himself; the same executioner dipped an iron spoon in the pot containing the boiling potion, which he poured liberally over each wound. Then the ropes that were to be harnessed to the horses were attached with cords to the patient's body; the horses were then harnessed and placed alongside the arms and legs, one at each limb. The cords had been tied so tightly by the men who pulled the ends that they caused him indescribable pain.

The horses tugged hard, each pulling straight on a limb, each horse held by an executioner. After a quarter of an hour, the same ceremony was repeated and finally, after several attempts, the direction of the horses had to be changed, thus: those at the arms were made to pull toward the head, those at the thighs toward the arms, which broke the arms at the joints. This was repeated several times without success. He [the condemned] raised his head and looked at himself...

This last operation was very long, because the horses used were not accustomed to drawing [being used to rip a living person's arms and legs off]; consequently, instead of four, six [horses] were needed; and when that did not suffice, they were forced, in order to cut off the wretch's thighs, to sever the sinews and hack at the joints....

Finally, the executioner, Samson, said ... that there was no way or hope of succeeding, and asked their Lordships if they wished him to have the prisoner cut into pieces. [A town official] ordered that renewed efforts be made, and this was done; but the horses gave up and one of those harnessed to the thighs fell to the ground. After two or three attempts, the executioner Samson and he who had used the pincers each drew out a knife from his pocket and cut the body at the thighs instead of severing the legs at the joints; the four horses gave a tug and carried off the two thighs after them, namely, that of the right side first, the other following; then the same was done to the arms, the shoulders, the arm-pits and the four limbs; the flesh had to be cut almost to the bone, the horses pulling hard carried off the right arm first and the other afterwards.

While this sounds a bit naive, successful politicians are mirrors of what their constituents want. Their positions on issues reflect back to us the very values we hold, or at least the values of those who vote. This is how politicians get elected. They will do exactly what we tell them to do if they wish to represent us in our communities, our states, and in Washington, D.C.

If there is not enough space for prisoners and, therefore, we must set some inmates free ensure each criminal has a turn to be in jail, then our nation is in serious trouble. This reasoning suggests that the states have discovered executing people is a way to deal with the misallocation of their financial resources. Simply put, this argument holds that we have no economic way to construct new prisons. Therefore, we have to execute those who we would put in prison if we could. Using this logic, our nation would certainly have a new way of dealing with overcrowding in public schools.

"But innocent children are different from killers," pointed out a young man in a Minnesota Vikings T-shirt. This led us to another common argument often cited in defense of the death penalty, the one that says murderers have forfeited their right to live and losing their own life is the only way they can truly "pay" for their crime. I sympathized with this argument, as it was essentially what I was thinking after I learned of Zane Floyd's rampage in the Las Vegas grocery store.

However, as a religious man, I also understand this argument from another perspective. Moses, with a great deal of help from God, parted a great sea, allowing his people to flee from Ramses the Great. Pharaoh's soldiers then chased Moses and his followers through the passage in the sea, only to have the sea crash in on them.

Are we supposed to feel bad for the Egyptians? Not really. Are we anti-Egyptian or anti-Pharaoh if we don't? No. The soldiers treated the Jews horribly and the offenders had many opportunities to stop their cruelty without incurring God's wrath. We are taught that the massive "execution," which occurred when the Red Sea smashed in on the soldiers after Moses' people went through it, was the Egyptian's fault for oppressing God's children. Thus, one could argue that the soldiers killed themselves with their own iniquities.

The reference to Moses is important because, as I pointed out to the class that day, many American laws are based on the Old Testament. That writing documents a broad array of severe punishments for breaking God's law, such as torture and public stoning. If we still used the same punishments that society employed thousands of years ago, as they still do in several countries around the world, then these occurrences would also be common in the streets of America. But they are not.

"There is a reason that these punishments don't happen in America," I asserted to my class. "We as a nation believe we have evolved morally, ethically, and judicially beyond those ancient practices. We don't sacrifice our children with knives, as Abraham was going to do. Similarly, we feel that some forms of punishment are just not acceptable."

To illustrate this to my Criminology class that day, I read out loud the following passage from the book Discipline and Punish, by Michele Foucault (Vintage Books, 1979). It describes a gruesome punishment once carried out on a man found guilty of stabbing King Louis XV of France in the late 1700s:

> The decree was that, "the flesh will be torn from his breasts, arms, thighs and calves with red-hot pincers, his right hand, holding the knife with which he committed the said parricide, burnt with sulfur, and, on those places where the flesh will be torn away, poured molten lead, boiling oil, burning

CHAPTER FOUR

Several years had passed between Edward Castro's first known knife attack in El Cajon, California, where he was defending himself in the bar fight, and the murder of Jason Miller in Euwella, Florida, though authorities strongly suspect he committed many other murders in between those two events. The length of time between Castro's first and second known attacks is not unusual for serial killers. Jeffery Dahmer, who murdered and ate 15 young boys, killed his first man after having sex with him in 1978. He then did not kill again until nine years later, in 1987. But once he resumed the killing, Dahmer regularly murdered young men until his arrest in July 1991. The multiyear lapse in killing certainly occurs in serial murder, and generally happens, as it did with both Castro and Dahmer, between the first and second victims.

But Castro's violent desires were clearly escalating and consuming him more and more. The time between the killing of Jason Miller and that of Robert Edwards was approximately two months. Yet less than 24 hours had passed since Edwards' murder when Castro planned to kill the stranger who gave him a ride to Ocala.

The initial shock of violently murdering an innocent person quickly passed for Castro. He could get money, sex, cars, and anything else he desired without worrying that a robbery or assault victim might give his description to the police. He soon realized that he enjoyed killing, that murder served his needs, both visceral and financial, very well.

He quickly overpowered Williams and, using his established method of attack, tied him up on the bed and told his incapacitated victim that he was going to kill him. Teasingly, Castro showed Williams a knife he had been hiding and began taunting him with it. Castro told the young man how he was going to stab him to death with the small blade. The terrified victim lay on the bed staring at the small knife in the hand of the violent sociopath, praying for some miracle to save his life.

Williams was a drifter, just like Castro, and had no money. Therefore, one can rule out robbery as a motive for Castro's desire to kill Richard Williams that day. It is more likely that Castro had discovered he enjoyed the thrill of killing other men. Once he recognized that horrible part of himself, he was willing to kill anyone he met, simply for the thrill it provided.

But rather than killing the teenager, Castro taunted him and talked about letting him go. Castro's behavior that day mirrored Larry Eyler's, who also had let some of his intended victims go, rather than killing them. It is likely that the young Williams did not appeal sexually to Castro in the way older men did. He may not have been overly aroused or sexually stimulated by the teenager.

Moments after teasing the teenager with the knife, Castro heard what he thought was Aaron Hernando returning to the apartment. Castro warned Williams to keep quiet about what had just happened. The terrified young man promised not to run or scream if he was untied, and Castro unleashed him from the bed. Although he would survive this encounter, Williams' descent into hell was just beginning.

Upon investigation, the two men learned that the noises they had heard were not those of Hernando coming home to the apartment. Instead, the clamor came from a drunk in the parking lot of the apartment complex. Steve Carter, a 56-year-old man from Ocala, was severely intoxicated, staggering near his parked car. Castro's lust for killing had been sparked by his attack on Williams, and seeing the drunken man with a car, Castro decided that Carter would be his next victim. He intended to use the man's car to get him out of Ocala, after he killed him to satisfy his hunger for death.

Castro calmly walked outside, introduced himself to the drunken stranger, and talked the man into coming inside the apartment and having a beer with him and the teenager from Iowa. Incredibly, Williams, whose life had just been threatened and very nearly taken, now chose to remain in the small apartment, drinking beer with his attacker.

While the two men and the youth laughed and drank together, Castro checked to see that he still had the small knife he used earlier to threaten Williams. He found that he did, but the killer wanted a larger knife to murder Carter. Castro left the two other men alone in the apartment and went to another unit in the complex to which he had access. There he found a seven-inch steak knife and hid the blade in his sock.

While walking back to Hernando's apartment, Castro saw his intended victim in his car, beginning to drive away from the apartment building. Carter may have begun to feel uncomfortable or scared, and decided to get out while Castro was gone. Or perhaps Williams, the victim who narrowly escaped a short time before, had warned the man of the danger. In either case, Carter had decided to quickly leave the apartment while his host was gone. Seeing his potential victim and get-away car about to drive off, Castro stopped Carter in an attempt to talk the man into returning to the apartment for another beer. Rather than follow his instincts and continue driving away, Carter agreed to come back inside with Castro. His decision to trust Castro and follow him back inside would cost him his life.

Back in the small apartment, the three men sat drinking on the bed. Surprisingly, Williams had not also tried to flee, as Carter did, while Castro was gone. Instead, he announced to the older men that he was going to take a shower. Williams probably knew what was about to happen to the inebriated Carter and did not wish to be in the room during the attack.

With Williams gone, Castro immediately grabbed Carter around the neck and began choking him. He throttled Carter with his bare hands to the point that blood began coming out of the victim's mouth and his face turned blue. With Carter nearly unconscious, Castro pulled the knife out of his sock and showed it to the gasping Carter telling him, "You are already dead, man ... Just accept it ... Don't even fight it, man ... You dig?"

Carter gasped for breath and held his hands at his burning throat. He tried to scream but his larynx was nearly crushed from the grip of the killer. Barely conscious, Steve Carter, who, moments before, had been safely in his car and about to drive away, stared into the face of his killer. Castro raised the steak knife in his right hand and began stabbing Steve Carter to death.

Unlike Castro's two previous murders in Florida and the incident with Williams earlier that day, Castro did not tie Carter to the bed or otherwise restrain him. As a result, when authorities found the murder scene, Carter's lifeless body had defensive stab wounds on his arms and hands where he had tried to protect himself during the attack. The wounds were inflicted with such strength that the blade of the knife actually went completely through Carter's arms, coming out the other side, at least three times. In the end, Carter was stabbed a total of 11 times, with the majority of the wounds concentrated on the left side of his chest. The force of Castro's attack on Carter was so vicious and intense that every wall, and even the ceiling, of the tiny bedroom was splattered with the blood that sprayed from the victim's severed arteries.

This was the scene, one of uncontrolled violence, which awaited Williams when he emerged from the shower. The shocked young man stood in the doorway staring at the carnage with a horrified look on his face. Castro, who was still in the room waiting for the teen, gave Williams a choice. He could either end up like the crumpled body lying right in front of him, or he could take Castro's bloody knife and stab the dead man, so that he, too, would be partly responsible for the murder. Castro knew that if Williams participated in the crime he would not call the police.

Contrary to what one might expect, it is not surprising that Castro did not murder Richard Williams to hide his crime of butchering Steve Carter. Often a killer attacks his victims to satisfy some lust or desire and will not have the desire to kill again so soon. In this sense, Castro was feeling satisfied immediately after the particularly bloody murder.

The terrified Williams faced an unimaginable dilemma. He could pick up the steak knife, which was slick with the still-warm blood of the man who moments ago was alive, and stab Carter's broken, bloodied corpse as Castro had done. Or, he could refuse to participate, flee the apartment, and try to outrun the killer. Such a tactic had not worked for Jason Miller, Castro's first known murder victim, months before.

Williams made his decision. He picked up the knife and repeatedly stabbed the dead man's body. Castro and Williams then cleaned themselves of Carter's blood and left the scene with the victim's car. Randomly, Castro selected Lake City, Florida, as his destination that day and set out with Williams to make the 80-mile journey. As they drove, Castro broke up the knife he had just used to kill

Steve Carter and threw it, piece by piece, out of the car window. To Castro, killing had become a way of life and he was not adversely affected by the horrific murder he had just committed.

But Williams had never seen a murder before, let alone taken part in one. One can only imagine his state of mind as he sat next to the man, who just two hours earlier had intended to kill him, then changed his mind and killed someone else instead. Perhaps he felt a sense of gratitude to Castro for sparing his life, and therefore had a perverse sense of loyalty to the murderer.

Or, as Castro himself liked to point out, the serial killer was charming and charismatic. He could get people to do things that he wanted them to do, even if the actions seemed horrible and revolting. Castro may have captivated Williams, the naive teenager, and the youth may have found himself drawn to this man who, with little thought about his actions, had the power of life and death over everyone with whom he came into contact.

While such an attraction to Castro might at first seem unusual, there are several cases in which a charismatic, cold-blooded killer captivated others and became a leader to his "followers." In 1978, the Reverend Jim Jones convinced approximately 650 adults and nearly 300 children to commit a mass murder and suicide that shocked and horrified the world. In the equally infamous case of the Manson family, Charles Manson persuaded his devotees to kill seven people in the Tate-LaBianca murders of 1969. In both instances, a charming and mysterious man compelled, influenced, and commanded his adoring followers to commit horrible atrocities to please him and show their devotion.

It is indeed likely that Richard Williams was under extreme mental strain and in a highly suggestive state. Castro had tied him up, psychologically tortured him, and then released him. Shortly afterward, Williams found his attacker standing over a blood-covered body and was forced to stab the corpse. The young man had experienced so much brutality, horror, and fear during the course of a few short hours, that he could not have been thinking clearly about his choice to continue traveling with Castro. Whatever thoughts filled the teenager's head, they must have been a horrified confusion beyond most people's understanding.

Once in Lake City, Florida, Castro and Williams drove around trying to come up with a way to scam some quick money. They approached a group of kids on the street and posed as drug dealers. The two claimed they had crack cocaine for sale, hoping to simply take the kids' money and leave. Instead, the youths told Castro and Williams that they didn't want drugs, so the two men drove off. When they left in their stolen car, in search of other victims to rob, the youngsters ran to a nearby pay phone and called the local police.

Minutes later Castro announced to Williams that he had to relieve himself, and he drove Steve Carter's car to a nearby gas station. When he emerged from the men's room, police cars had surrounded the stolen vehicle. All of the rage and violent lust that had driven the serial killer for the last few months came crashing down, and Castro knew that an end had come to his disturbed life on the street.

Upon seeing the police cars, Castro assumed that officers were there to arrest him for the murders. While standing in the parking lot of the gas station, he immediately confessed to the three killings. In actuality, the police knew nothing about the murders and wanted simply to question Williams and Castro about harassing the kids down the street. After his arrest, Castro commented that had he had a gun when he exited the men's room, he would have

"When the four limbs had been pulled away, the confessors came to speak to him; but his executioner told them that he was dead, though the truth was that I saw the man move, his lower jaw moving from side to side as if he were talking. One of the executioners even said shortly afterwards that when they had lifted the trunk to throw it on the stake, he was still alive. The four limbs were untied from the ropes and thrown on the stake set up in the enclosure in line with the scaffold, then the trunk and the rest were covered with logs and faggots, and fire was put to the straw mixed with this wood.

After members of the class had sufficiently recovered from the horrific passages I had read, we discussed another theory. If such tortures were applied to each and every person who voluntarily took the life of another human being, and if those tortures were common public spectacles, would we see a decrease in the rate of murder? I argued that if gruesome punishments were applied to every murderer, the practice would probably deter others from committing pre-meditated murder. They would not prevent all murders, but they would prevent pre-meditated murder.

Criminologists define pre-meditated murder as one in which the killer plans out his or her attack, has the opportunity to refrain from taking the life of another, is of sound mind, and willingly and intentionally hurts and injures another person with the intent of killing him. For those killings that are planned out, severe public torture and death would probably decrease their incidence.

One problem: Crimes of passion, which make up most murders in the United States, are not pre-meditated and would not be stopped by simply watching public executions. Crimes of passion, by their nature, are crimes in which the murder was not thought out or planned by the killer. If a majority of murders are not pre-meditated, but are instead committed in a fit of anger or violent passion by someone who has never killed before, the killer does not weigh the costs and benefits of his actions. He is not likely to stop and think before he pulls the trigger. Instead homicide often results from a panicked thief or an angry spouse who, for lack of a better term, "snaps" and kills a person.

I then proposed to the students that to serve as an effective deterrent to murder, every member of society would have to view the violent and bloody executions, and every person who commits murder would have to suffer that punishment. This would include young children, since our society has seen cases of children as young as 5 or 6 years old who commit murder. Further, we would have to find an executioner who was willing to violently torture small children to death in public, because at times, they are killers, too.

By this time in the class discussion, it was obvious that the students who opposed the death penalty had found new arguments to support their views. Alternatively, the students who were in favor of the death penalty had become frustrated and angry. To be fair, and to explore all sides of the issue, I then switched sides and began making arguments as to why the death penalty should be used in America.

First, I pointed out that our criminal justice system in America uses increasing levels of punishment for crimes of increasing severity. For example, most people would be outraged if they heard of a person who was sentenced to 15 years in prison for shoplifting. The punishment simply doesn't fit the crime.

However, in the case of a habitual drunk driver who is repeatedly arrested for driving under the influence of alcohol and then finally crashes his car into a family walking on the sidewalk killing them all, a 15-year sentence would be more socially acceptable. This crime was more severe and the drunk was a repeat offender. Thus, as the crimes increase in severity, the punishments must also escalate in order for us to consider them appropriate.

"But why can't murderers spend the rest of their lives in prison?" offered one young man who opposed the death penalty.

One student presented the argument that keeping convicted criminals in prison for life is so expensive for taxpayers, that, in the interest of economics, our government should use the death penalty more often. This sounded to me like a type of controlled, economic Darwinism. Those that failed in our society were "selected out" to create financial benefits for the rest of us.

"One problem with this position," I argued, "is that it starts a process of debating how much a person's life is worth. I don't mean in the philosophical sense, where the moral value of humanity is questioned. I mean it much more literally." I proposed to the class that if we used economics as the gauge of human life, we would each have to justify our existence financially. We would have to prove that we are contributing more to the economy than we are taking from it.

But I pointed out a different flaw in the first student's argument, if one follows the logic that the penalty should fit the crime. "What about all those other offenses that can land a person in jail for life? A criminal who commits multiple counts of kidnapping, rape, attempted murder, and other violent offenses gets thrown in jail with no hope of being released. If murder is the most severe type of crime, what additional step could be taken to show that it is more severe than multiple counts of kidnapping or rape?"

Other students blurted out the answer, "Death."

"But that's so horrible!" objected a young woman.

"Sure the punishment is horrible," I volleyed back. "That's the point. Their crime was the most horrible crime that one can commit, and the punishment should be equally severe and horrible. The offender's crime was so atrocious that their death is the only way they can truly pay for the life they took." After all, in practice, murderers are the only criminals executed anymore in the United States. By willingly taking the life of another person, haven't they forfeited their own right to live?

I referred to an example from the state of Florida. In a 1999 Florida Supreme Court ruling, Judge Clarence T. Johnson, Jr. stated,

> Execution inherently involves fear, and it may involve some degree of pain. That pain may include pain associated with affixing straps around the head and body to secure the head and body in the electric chair. However, any pain associated therewith is necessary to ensure that the integrity of the execution process is maintained.

"Everyone knows that being executed is supposed to be scary and painful," I argued. I looked around the room to see contemplative, and, sometimes, confused faces. I pressed on to the final question that I intended to pose to my students that day.

"Could you watch an execution?"

Blank faces looked back at me.

I clarified the question and tried again. "Not a public execution where you are one of hundreds or thousands of people," I explained, "but a modern execution, where they hook the offender up to an electric cable and fry him. Or where they put him in a room full of cyanide gas until he chokes to death. Could you watch that?"

The students sat quietly pondering the question. I studied their expressions, trying to gauge their response. Some of them looked puzzled; others appeared surprised. One girl looked bored and glanced up at the clock on the wall behind me.

I turned around and saw that we were out of time. "OK, that's it for today. We will pick up there next time," I announced. The sound of notebooks snapping closed and chairs scraping the floor filled the room as students began heading for the door. But not all of them were so eager to leave for the day. Several students approached me after the class to ask about my personal feelings on the death penalty.

I found it difficult to answer their questions. I had certainly thought about it at length, and it was a question that I considered important enough to warrant an answer. Yet I was unclear in my response. In spite of my professional and personal exposure to the issues of the death penalty, I had not been forced to take a position one way or the other.

"I am not totally sure," I confessed to them. "I keep changing my mind on the issue." At that point, I had not yet seen anything that compelled me to make up my mind.

CHAPTER EIGHT

Edward Castro was born on Jan. 26, 1950, in El Centro, California. Earlier that same day, on the other side of the world, an announcement was made that the Republic of India had been created. Following the benevolent Mohandas Gandhi, India had found peace through one of the greatest non-violent struggles the world had ever known. Thousands of miles away, a boy entered that same world. But this child would soon find that his entire life would be a struggle met, and ultimately lost, with violence.

During the first two years of Edward Castro's life, he lived with his father and mother, a chronic alcoholic, in a physically abusive environment. The marriage between the child's parents was volatile and violent, and it only worsened when the adults were drinking. As an infant, Edward was developmentally disabled. He did not learn to walk until he was 2-years-old. The toddler also had numerous health problems, and his early childhood was marked with repeated hospitalizations for conditions as diverse as dehydration and gastrointestinal disorders.

The relationship between his parents ended when Edward was 2-years-old. At that time, his mother sent the child and his siblings to live with family and friends in Tijuana, Mexico. There, Edward was again beaten and physically abused by his guardians. Edward's uncle also repeatedly sodomized the boy, in addition to the physical beatings he suffered at the hands of other adults. Further, those charged with the toddler's care began, as a joke, making him consume large quantities of alcohol, which invariably stunts mental and social development in young children. This pattern of ongoing physical abuse and neglect, to which Edward Castro was subjected, is common in the early lives of those individuals who go on to become serial killers.

Criminologists have attempted to explain this connection between continuous sexual and physical abuse experienced during childhood and acts of violence later in life. One theory suggests that the savage deeds committed as an adult are an attempt by the offender to get rid of his or her past, or to redirect it onto someone else. While this may sound unusual, it is far from uncommon in the arena of human behavior. A similar belief and action has become common in South Africa over the last few years. There, men with AIDS often believe that having sex with a virgin girl will cure them of the deadly virus. They imagine they are passing the AIDS virus from their body to the young woman's. The younger the rape victim, the greater the chance that she is a virgin, and therefore, the more likely she is to be able to help rid them of their disease. Consequently, this "cure" has resulted in an enormous number of rape cases with elementary-school-aged victims.

Learning Theory, which is discussed in most books on criminological theory, has been offered by experts as another way to explain why people who become serial killers were often abused as children. Learning Theory maintains that physically abused children imitate the behavior they saw as youngsters. Then, as adults, they act out what they learned from their parents. Some believe that adults who are violent and anti-social learned that total disregard for other people from their parents. Thus, they simply practiced what *they* were taught. They learned by example that violence and sexual abuse are acceptable ways to get the things they need from other people.

Regardless of the theory, countless cases suggest a connection between childhood abuse and violent behavior as an adult. One well-known example of a serial killer that suffered from horrible child abuse is Henry Lee Lucas, who claimed to have murdered as many as 300 people from 1959 until his arrest in 1983.

As a child, Lucas lived with his mother, who was a chronic alcoholic and a prostitute. On several occasions his mother would bring home her male customers and have sex with the strangers in front of the child. She also liked to dress young Henry up like a girl and beat him so severely that at times he was left unconscious from the encounter. One attack on the child by his mother, with a wooden board, was so viscous that Henry sustained a fractured skull.

His mother's extreme violence and open sexuality certainly made an impact on Henry Lucas and how he viewed other people. He saw no value in humanity and no love or compassion in his emotional or familial bonds. As he began to mature into a young teen, Lucas desperately sought sexual contact in an attempt to understand it and to become physically intimate with *anyone* or *anything*, just to get a sense of closeness. His confusion and desperation for reassurance and intimacy grew until he began having sex with his older brother.

Soon the troubled youth began to combine his abnormal sexual desires with the violent tendencies that he had learned from his mother. The resulting deeds clearly indicated a frightened and desperate young man. For example, he repeatedly tortured to death small animals and then had sexual intercourse with their dead bodies. This appalling act gave Henry Lucas feelings of power, as well as provided him with sexual gratification.

By 1959, the 23-year-old man had a history of assault and burglary. Many criminologists, including this author, believe such offenses are often precursors to sexual crimes, since both involve the violation of another person or their intimate surroundings. Lucas had clearly learned to think of other people as tools or instruments that could be used for whatever purpose one desired.

One evening in 1959, Lucas and his mother, who was 74 years old at that point, got into a vicious argument. The years of abuse, sexual depravity, and physical, sexual and emotional torture in Henry's life culminated in a violent rage. The dispute resulted in the young man stabbing his mother to death. But, despite the gory murder, Henry still did not feel that this woman had been punished enough for the abuse he suffered at her hands. To help him feel that her punishment wouldn't stop with death, he then repeatedly raped her corpse.

For the next 24-four years, Henry Lee Lucas traveled around the country killing and torturing random victims until he was arrested in 1983. After his arrest, the serial killer confessed to murdering 300 people. Later he recanted that number and claimed that he had been exaggerating.

Both Lucas and Castro suffered abuse that began at very young ages, when their undeveloped minds were first learning the complex nature of social relationships. Sociologists and child psychologists have recognized for decades that between the ages of 2 and 5, children learn to view themselves and their actions according to how they will affect others. In these early years children also learn to trust and respect others, as well as themselves. They learn to share, to be kind, to love, to forgive, to communicate, to be proud of themselves for their accomplishments, and to work with others. They begin to learn that some of their behaviors are right and some are wrong.

In these formative years, children learn that their actions can have negative consequences for both themselves and other people. They also begin to learn, mostly from their parents, that their every want and desire cannot be fulfilled. In a healthy family, the child learns that he can feel loved, appreciated and worthwhile even if he can't have every piece of candy in the checkout lane at the grocery store. This stage of social and emotional development is, by far, the most significant in a person's life.

In no uncertain terms, it is during those years that children begin to learn to see themselves as "social" beings, rather than as "solitary." They are required to live by rules and restrictions that, at times, are contrary to their immediate desires. If, during those years, the child is severely and physically punished, without a reason that he can understand, he will begin to see himself as alone, afraid, and worthless to the adult. During these years, children are also desperately trying to please the adults in their lives.

Eventually, children of abuse lose trust in adults. They begin to believe that what is said to them may not necessarily be the truth, and certainly is not in the child's best interest. In short, the child will learn to fear the adult, the punishment, and the abuse, but will not learn that his actions affect anyone but himself. Once started down this road, he is well on his way to becoming what sociologists refer to as a sociopath, and his parents and/or guardians have contributed significantly to his pathology.

A sociopath, by definition, does not care about the emotions or feelings of another person. He lives his life thinking only of himself and his immediate wants and desires. The pain, suffering, fear, and humiliation that he forces on others are unimportant or largely irrelevant to him. In fact, a sociopath often enjoys the anguish he causes his victims, and is often sexually aroused by the violence. A sociopath is frequently a compulsive liar who will cheat, steal from, or harm another person to satisfy himself. The age-old saying "do unto others as you would have done unto you" does not enter the mind of the sociopath and has no bearing on his behavior.

While the term "psychopath" is often used in the films, books and the media to denote the worst kind of predatory monster, a "sociopath" is actually much more frightening. In fact, the suffix "-path" comes from a Greek word meaning "diseased" or "suffering." Thus, *socio*path describes a person whose view of society and social interactions is diseased. The sociopath's disease originates from outside himself, in his interactions with the outside world. He sees all other people, including lovers, family, friends and strangers, simply as tools to get what he wants or as playthings purely for his pleasure. Castro, Lucas, and John Wayne Gacey (who will be discussed later) were all sociopaths. However, so were Castro's uncle, Lucas's mother, and Gacey's father.

The case of a 41-one-year-old pedophile that I interviewed further demonstrates the sociopathic mind. This man had engaged in a series of homosexual encounters with two boys, aged 12 and 13. In my interviews with him, the offender described the "love" he had for young boys. He claimed that these children were his every desire and dreams come true. He described feelings of strength and importance when he had sexual contact with them, and commented that he couldn't understand why those feelings were wrong and why he was being treated like a criminal.

I tried to explain to this man that it was not possible for a 12 or 13-year-old boy to be involved in a romantic relationships with a middle-age, adult man. The children, whether the offender understood it or not, were scared, overpowered, and were being taken advantage of by the adult. The criminal gently smiled and said, as though he was talking to a child, "That just isn't true."

This pedophile was exhibiting sociopathic tendencies. He simply could not see that the young boys did not enjoy the behavior that gave him such intense sexual gratification. He could not recognize that the boys felt dominated and overpowered by a full-grown adult male, and that the encounters were really rape, rather than consensual sex. This sociopath was so interested in his own desires, feelings, and satisfaction, that he refused to even consider that his deeds were painful and destructive for the two children. To satisfy his own sexual desires, he destroyed these children's lives, seriously harming them emotionally and psychologically, and shattering the boys' ability to trust other people. Sociopaths, like this offender, are often victims themselves as children, and are raised in abusive, traumatic and dangerous environments.

On the other hand, psychopaths can have perfectly happy and healthy childhoods, and then at some point in their life, suffer a major psychological breakdown. They may become delusional, highly paranoid, or lose all understanding of reality. *Psycho*pathic literally means there is a disease in their *psyche,* or brain.

Psychopathic murderers generally don't become serial killers. Since they seldom see the world, or themselves, in a factual manner, their ability to avoid capture by the police is non-existent. The psychopath may not even try to escape punishment, since he often does not realize what he is doing. Therefore, he frequently makes no effort to avoid detection, leaving behind incriminating evidence, such as fingerprints or victims who can identify their attacker. Clearly, Castro was not a psychopath. He fled the cities where he had committed a murder and even hid out in an alcohol rehabilitation clinic, indicating that he understood his actions and knew society viewed those actions as wrong.

The psychopath commonly kills because he thinks he must. He may believe that God is commanding him to murder. Alternatively, a psychopath may attack another because in his delusional mind he believes that the victim is trying to kill or hurt him. To the psychopath, it truly seems that if he doesn't defend himself, the victim will attack and kill him. He may believe this even if the victim is a child or an invalid. Clearly, a psychopath does not understand what he is doing and often hates himself for "having to kill" the victim. In contrast, the sociopath simply kills because it makes him feel good.

Different forces drive the sociopath and the psychopath. While the psychopath typically feels guilty and is ashamed of what he has done, a sociopath never feels remorse for his crimes. The sociopath kills to fulfill some deep-rooted need or fantasy in himself. He ultimately kills for his own pleasure. However, a psychopath might insist he received instructions to kill other people, commands from some other planet or spirit. In the criminal justice system, this distinction is important.

Psychopaths are seldom executed for the crimes they commit because they are not fully responsible for their actions. A recent and well-publicized example of this occurred in the case of Andrea Yates in Texas. The mother systematically murdered her five small children by drowning them in the family's bathtub, in order to "save them." A jury later found her guilty of multiple counts of capital murder. The District Attorney and the judge concluded that Yates was bordering on insanity at the time she killed her children, and, therefore, should not be executed. This insanity determination overrode the fact that the murders were pre-mediated and they essentially involved the torture of children. The presence of torture and premeditation in a murder trial generally results in a death sentence in the state of Texas, but it did not for Andrea Yates.

The case of Ed Gein demonstrates another example of how psychopaths receive more lenient sentences than do sociopaths in our criminal justice system. In Plainfield, Wisconsin, this particular offender murdered and mutilated women during the 1950s. Perhaps what made Gein most infamous was his practice of making what he called a "woman suit" out of the skin from the body of his victim. With the dead skin, his "suit," over his face and naked body, he would walk around his farmhouse pretending to be a woman. Gein also decorated his house with human body parts, including a chair constructed of human arms and a lampshade made from human skin.

Gein was caught when he murdered the mother of the Sheriff's Deputy of Plainfield and did very little to avoid detection by the police. When arrested, the serial killer chatted openly about the murders he had committed, and also told police how he adorned himself with the unique "decorations" afterwards. Ed Gein claimed that he didn't understand what all the uproar was about, as if this practice of his were quite ordinary. During the questioning, he appeared very mild-mannered and detached from the environment around him. Psychiatrists soon determined Gein to be insane, and thus psychopathic, not sociopathic. As psychopaths are generally not viewed as mentally capable and directly responsible for their crimes, he spent the rest of his life in a psychiatric hospital, rather than going to prison. Had the system determined Gein to be aware of his surroundings—his acts and the consequences of what he was doing, making him sociopathic rather than psychopathic—his punishment would have been spending his life in a maximum security prison rather than an insane asylum. Reportedly, Ed Gein appeared content with his life in the asylum, and supposedly enjoyed playing board games and dancing with the nurses until he died in 1984.

Marshall Applewhite, the leader of the Heaven's Gate religious cult in San Diego, California, provides a more recent example of a psychopath. In March 1997, Applewhite and 38 of his followers "left their mortal bodies" by killing themselves with a combination of sedatives and vodka mixed into applesauce. This man believed that an alien spaceship hid within the tail of the Hale-Bopp comet, and that he and his followers would reach eternal salvation through this extra-terrestrial vehicle if they all committed suicide together. He preached these ideas to his followers and was directly responsible for the deaths of 38 other people. From the videotapes of his sermons, investigators concluded that Applewhite was psychotic. He had a false perception of reality and lectured his notions to his devotees. Applewhite didn't kill his followers for a sexual thrill, as would a sociopath. Instead he helped to kill them so that they could all become "exalted" and reach deliverance. This distinction made his behavior, and hence his crime, one of psychopathy rather than sociopathy.

A person that becomes a sociopathic killer begins as all children begin: innocent, pure, hopeful, and wanting nothing but love, comfort, and reassurance. But some children are never given those basic needs and are instead tortured, abused and horribly punished. The result is, at times, a person who has been *forced* to think only of himself and who has a natural mistrust and anger toward others. This is the sociopath, and this is exactly what Edward Castro, the serial killer in Florida, had become.

The sociopathic killer is much more dangerous than is the psychopath. Once he begins killing, he is unlikely to stop until authorities apprehend him. Such was the case of John Wayne Gacey. As with Henry Lee Lucas and Edward Castro, Gacey's early life was spent living with an abusive and alcoholic parent. Gacey's father was an alcoholic who severely beat John's mother. The man also physically and emotionally abused John as a child. Ironically, the only son in the family adored his abusive father and wanted desperately to please him.

Gacey's mother, herself a victim of the abuse, took out her anger and frustration on John. Throughout his childhood, she reportedly gave her son enemas for no reason. These were, of course, humiliating and disturbing to the young man, but his mother continued to give them to make herself feel better as a parent. In her mind, she was "caring for him."

His mother, who was regularly abused and humiliated by John's father, began to abuse and humiliate her child in an attempt to make herself feel better. The rationale is, "If I am hurting and in pain, my hurt and pain will *seem* better to me if I hurt someone else worse." John Wayne Gacey eventually also adopted this twisted logic. He began sodomizing young men in an attempt to feel stronger and more complete as a man.

In the mid-1970s, young boys began disappearing around the Chicago neighborhood where Gacey lived. As a man known to have a sexual attraction to young boys, Gacey was repeatedly questioned by police about the disappearances. But authorities could find no evidence connecting Gacey to any abduction until Dec. 13, 1978. At that time, police obtained a search warrant and entered Gacey's home to look for clues in the disappearance of boys that had worked for the man. Eventually, police found the bodies of 33 young men and boys buried in the crawl space under Gacey's home. During his confession, the killer tried to defend himself by claiming that several of the boys were trying to use him and blackmail him. In an attempt to pass himself off as insane, Gacey told police that he killed the victims to protect himself from them. This approach failed. Before being executed by lethal injection, John Wayne Gacey gave many interviews to the media. He often expressed his love and admiration for his father and mother. Clearly Gacey inflicted pain and suffering on others to feel better about himself.

Edward Castro's evolution into a sociopathic serial killer also began in his childhood years. After being severely psychologically and physically abused by adults for two years in Tijuana, Mexico, the small boy was sent back to the United States to live with his mother. There, the beatings, neglect and sexual abuse resumed again, this time even more severely. The young child, barely 4 years old, was raped and sexually assaulted by members of his own family.

The young Edward Castro endured numerous, painful sexual assaults as a child. He was forced to engage in sex with adults as well as to have sex with his sister, for the cruel enjoyment of his uncle. The man would watch the two children carry out his own depraved sexual desires.

As Castro grew from a toddler into a school-age child, the physical maltreatment also became more severe. When Edward was only 6 years old, his uncle took the quiet, nervous little boy, who had already been horribly sexually assaulted, and slammed the trunk of a car on the child's head. As one would imagine, Edward began having horrible nightmares and severe headaches after this incident. The symptoms continued for two years, when at the age of 8, another adult, his baby-sitter, began molesting him.

For young Edward, the family, and thus the world, was a horrible, painful, and humiliating place. Instead of loving and nurturing the child, his caregivers hurt him in the most severe way possible, just to please themselves. This is where Edward Castro's cruelty and sexual perversion began.

Edward became a nervous and withdrawn child. He later dropped out of high school and joined the Marine Corps, in search of self-respect. In the Marines, Castro became an alcoholic, as his mother had been. His alcohol abuse would continue until his eventual imprisonment for murder.

After a mere five months in the Marine Corps, the 18-year-old Castro deserted the military and fled to Canada. Soon after crossing the border, he was arrested and imprisoned on charges of grand theft auto. After completing his short jail sentence, he was immediately arrested by FBI agents for deserting the United States military. For this, Edward Castro served six months in a federal penitentiary.

In the ten years following his release from prison, Castro had several relationships with different women. After fathering two children, both boys, Castro decided he wanted to give up booze and "go straight." His attempt at sobriety and a normal life ended within a year, when he once again began drinking, this time even more heavily. It was during this period in the young man's life that he first exhibited signs of violence and anti-social tendencies. On multiple occasions when he was drinking, Castro became involved in violent fistfights. About this time, he also suffered another serious brain injury in an automobile accident and began having blackouts soon afterward.

When the mother of his two sons divorced him, Castro's behavior became even more erratic. The abandonment drove the fitful man into an even further state of mental instability. Distraught and depressed, he turned his violent impulses inward on himself and slashed his wrists. Undoubtedly, to him, his life seemed one of pain and frustration. His only solace, alcohol, numbed him and drove him deeper into despair. One year after his failed suicide attempt, the 29-year-old Castro entered an alcohol rehabilitation program. But the treatment failed to end his craving for intoxication, and he began drinking again.

Over the next seven years, those leading up to the series of murders in Florida, Castro drank more heavily and fell further into mental illness and anti-social behavior. It was during this period that Edward suffered a crushing head injury from a lead pipe during a fight. While injured, he stabbed the assailant. Soon after this incident, Castro began exhibiting strange behavior. After an alcohol-induced blackout, he would often take on a completely different personality and refer to himself as "Tony."

After his arrest for the murder of Steve Carter, physicians gave Castro a full physical and mental evaluation. Psychiatrists concluded that the killer suffered from post-traumatic stress disorder, a result of the extensive sexual assault Castro experienced throughout his childhood. Doctors reported that he also had poor impulse control, maladapted behavior, and depression. His mental problems, which were reported by physicians as being "severe," stemmed directly from his repeated sexual abuse and extreme physical abuse as a child that caused numerous brain injuries.

Edward Castro was, without a doubt, a malicious killer. But his parents and the dysfunctional environment he grew up in created this monster. They gave Castro his distorted view of the world. As in the cases of Henry Lee Lucas and John Wayne Gacey, Edward Castro's sociopathy can be linked, at least in part, to the abuse he suffered during his childhood. At one point, even if it seems a lifetime ago, the cruel, evil man was simply a scared, little boy who did not want to be hurt anymore.

It should be noted that while all three men were sociopaths, they still acted freely and killed their victims voluntarily. Sociologists can easily point to childhood experiences that contributed to the sociopathy of the killers, yet each one ultimately made his own decision to use other human beings as tools, meat, or playthings. Parents may give a child all the reasons in the world to become sociopathic, but the individual ultimately decides if he will, or will not, harm other people. The accountability remains with the killer, regardless of the environment in which he grew up. While the serial killer is responsible, he isn't the only person responsible for the murders he committed. In the end, Castro still had his free will. He did not have to commit the vicious murders that he did.

Regardless of how he became one, Edward Castro was a serial killer. In criminological terms, a "serial killing" or "serial murder" is a pattern of homicides that occur at different places over a period of time. While sexual deviation is not necessarily required for a person to be considered a serial murderer, criminologists often add the element of sexual attraction as one motivation for the killings.

For example, we would not typically consider a gang member, who commits five drive-by shootings over a period of three years, to be a serial killer. Generally, gang-related murders are carried out for revenge, disputed territory, or illegal drug activity. However, most experts would consider a man, who abducts, rapes and murders five women over the same three-year period, to be a serial killer. Unlike the gang member, this killer attacks for sexual gratification, power, and for the thrill that stealing another person's life brings. But more than the sexual element differentiates the two types of killers. A gang member kills to resolve some issue or conflict, but for the serial killer, murder itself is the goal.

To further illustrate this, I was interviewing a former street-gang member who had murdered two people and had attempted to kill a third. He was also an accomplice in one pre-meditated homicide and one attempted murder. All this occurred over a period of four years, yet the young man would not be considered a serial killer, because of his motivation for the crimes.

In one of our interviews, I asked him how he felt when he "shot at" someone. He replied that "it wasn't hard," and said that he didn't get upset afterward. He further explained, "If I didn't shoot them, they woulda did me. I mean, they weren't innocent, they woulda did the same thing." He went on to describe how shooting someone in another gang is like a type of preventive self-defense, where you take him out before he threatens to harm you.

Clearly this man was a callused killer, with absolutely no remorse for his series of murders. Yet, he was still not what we call a "serial killer." Sexual gratification or power did not motivate him. Killing was, in his mind, a way to survive on the streets, and was not an end, in and of itself.

For murders to be regarded as part of a "serial killing," they must be separated by some length of time, must occur at different locations, and the killer must be thrilled or otherwise stimulated by his acts. Edward Castro's first known murder was that of Jason Miller, in Euwella, Florida. The crime was not well-planned and his victim nearly escaped alive, by running outside the trailer. But Castro quickly learned from his mistakes and improved on his killing methods. He discovered that being a serial killer satisfied both his violent, homosexual desires and his need for money. Once Castro started killing, it quickly became his preferred method for acquiring his day-to-day necessities, and for satisfying his inner sexual demons.

While police suspect that Edward Castro was responsible for several murders before his spree in Florida, including one in El Cajon, California, one in New Orleans, Louisiana, and one in Red Bluff, California, he was never formally charged with those crimes. During his confession, Castro offered little information about his involvement in the murders in other states, but willingly talked at length about the killing of Miller, Edwards, and Carter over a three-month period that fall in Florida. He repeatedly stated that it felt good to finally get it all out in the open and "off his chest." He also remarked that in the end, he believed he was ready to get caught. It seemed that even Edward Castro, the hardened sociopathic killer, had a limit to how much death and brutality he could bear.

CHAPTER NINE

On Dec. 1, 2000, I was in my office at the university visiting with a student named Matt, who had taken several of my classes over the last two semesters. Matt led an adventurous and exciting life, traveling the world, while still managing to score higher on exams than most other students in my classes. It was shortly after 1:00 on a Friday afternoon. In about 30 minutes, I was scheduled to teach a section of Introduction to Sociology to a group of students that did not want to sit through a Friday afternoon class.

During my conversation with Matt, my computer announced the arrival of an e-mail message. I glanced at the monitor and was startled when I read the subject line of the new message: "Impending Execution." I noticed that the sender was from Florida. Without reading any further, I had a sick feeling that I already knew what the message was about.

My stomach muscles tensed and I mumbled "Oh, no." My facial expressions and the tone of my voice must have alarmed Matt. He curiously asked, "What? What is it?" I didn't answer him, but I thought to myself that the letter I had written months before and then forgotten, was about to become a very important part of my life.

To my surprise, the message was short. It simply stated that the Florida State Prison in Starke did not have my home phone number and would like me to call them with it right away. With my heart racing and my hands slightly shaking, I dialed the phone number given in the e-mail. After two rings, the Administrative Assistant to the Warden answered and the following conversation occurred:

Ms. Harper-	"Hello, Florida State Prison."
Me-	"Hello, this is Dr. Joseph Diaz in Minnesota, I just received an e-mail asking me to call this number right away."
Ms. Harper-	In a friendly and conversational tone, "Yes, hello, Dr. Diaz, how are you today?"
Me-	Cautiously, after a pause, "I'm fine, how is everything down there?"
Ms. Harper-	"Oh, fine, thank you. We didn't have your home number on your letter, so we wanted to get that from you, if possible."
Me-	"Uh ... sure. You mean my letter from this summer? Sure, OK" I then gave her my home telephone number.
Ms. Harper-	"OK, thank you, Doctor. We needed that for our records."
Me-	"Sure, I understand. Sorry I didn't include it with the letter."
Ms. Harper-	"Oh, that's all right. We have two executions scheduled for next week, one on Thursday and one on Friday. Which one would you like to watch?"

Very seldom do I find myself unable to state my opinion or vocalize my feelings on a particular matter. But in this case, the friendly, conversational tone of the warden's assistant at the beginning of the phone conversation caused me to relax and let up my guard. I began to think that the phone call was not regarding an execution, and when I heard her last question, I was totally unprepared for it. It would be like going in to a physician's office and hearing the following:

Physician-   With a big, friendly smile on his face, "Well, your tests are back and we have some good news! You don't have strep throat."

Patient-   With a relaxing sigh of relief, "Whew! I'm so glad, I didn't want to go through that. Thank you very much."

Physician-   "You're welcome. However you *do* have an advanced form of cancer and will probably be dead within the month."

My first thought was, "Florida is executing *two* inmates in a 24-hour period?" That's more executions than most countries in the world have had in the last 24 years. I was shocked. It seemed so practical and clinical, almost as if they thinking, "Well, the death machine is already warmed up. Let's save some time and use it again before it cools down and has to be restarted."

The assistant on the phone was asking me which of the two executions I wanted to watch. *Wanted* to watch. I don't think I *wanted* to watch someone be executed at all, but that was how she phrased it.

Soon I found myself asking her about the individuals who were scheduled to die. I asked her to tell me about the two prisoners and I felt a bit like a restaurant patron asking the waiter which dish to try. Ms. Harper told me that both prisoners were men convicted of murder (which I had already assumed), and that she really couldn't tell me anything else because it would violate their privacy. The irony seemed lost on her. I could watch their death, but couldn't know about their lives.

I asked their names and was told that "the prisoner" (not man, but "prisoner") scheduled for Thursday was named Edward Castro and the prisoner scheduled (not "scheduled to die," but simply "scheduled") for Friday was named Robert Ruger. I couldn't answer right away which day I wanted to go, or, more correctly, I couldn't decide right away who I wanted to watch die, so I didn't say anything at all. She must have taken my silence as a question of protocol, because she began telling me about the time to show up at the prison and how to dress. I learned that "professional dress" was required, though I didn't know what "professional" meant in this context.

We were now about one or two minutes into the phone call, and I still had not made up my mind about whose death I would watch, Castro's or Ruger's, or even if I could watch *any* execution. While trying to decide, I began thinking about the men's names. The first was Edward Castro. I bet that it was difficult for someone with the name "Castro" to be given a fair trial in the State of Florida. The second man's name, Ruger, is a type of handgun, used by both murderers and police officers all over the country. What a choice!

"I don't mean to sound callous," I began, "but it is going to be expensive for me to come down to Florida with only six or seven days notice. What happens if I make the trip and there is no execution?"

After asking the question, it occurred to me that she might interpret my question to mean, "Well if I'm coming all the way down there, you'd better kill somebody!" Instead, what I really wanted to know was how to adjust my expectations. Should I definitely plan for the execution to occur? Or was it possible that I might make the trek and, after an intense wait, find out that no execution was going to happen. It just seemed like such an emotional process to go through the whole mental preparation for no reason.

Ms. Harper made the impossible decision easier by telling me that Ruger, the second inmate scheduled to die had just hired a new lawyer. The convicted killer was fighting for a stay of execution. She explained that this meant a possible postponement of his execution was likely. Generally, the postponements of executions are only for a month, but I guess when you are about to die, you take whatever you can get.

Edward Castro, on the other hand, had gone to the Florida Supreme Court seeking permission to fire his attorneys so that they would *stop* the appeals process. In other words, Ruger was fighting to delay his execution, and Castro was fighting to make sure that his happened as soon as possible.

Much to my surprise, and embarrassment, I found myself asking Ms. Harper if I could, seeing as how I was traveling so far from Minnesota to Florida, watch both men die, one on Thursday and the other on Friday. I was horrified at myself once the question was out of my mouth. When I came to work that morning I was not planning to watch anyone be executed, and now I was proposing to watch two men be killed within a 24-hour period.

Ms. Harper responded professionally that watching two different people be executed, "back to back," was not allowed for several reasons. While she did not elaborate, I'm now sure that one reason must have been that the witness probably could not psychologically handle so much death in such a short period of time. She did compromise, however, and said that that if for some reason the Castro execution wasn't carried out on Thursday, the warden would give me permission to be present during the Ruger execution the next day. So it was decided. Of the two men on the brink of death, I would watch Edward Castro die.

However, my involvement with the Ruger case was not yet over.

CHAPTER TEN

After promising to call the warden's assistant if I had any questions over the next few days, I hung up the phone and looked in Matt's direction. By listening to my side of the conversation, he had figured out the story. "So are you going to do it? Are you going to watch an execution?" he wanted to know.

"Yeah, I guess so," I replied, but not so confidently. "I mean, it makes me sick, but maybe I should go. Or maybe not. I don't know, I mean ... I just don't know." Suddenly I found myself unprepared for what I had volunteered to do when I wrote those letters months before. I had no idea how I was supposed to act and what I was supposed to do.

I looked at the clock and realized that my class was about to start and I was going to be late. I numbly walked down the hall to the classroom, feeling slightly drunk and dizzy. With the semester all but over, my students probably thought they had heard all they could about female genital mutilation, suicide, homicide, rape, serial murder, and violence in street gangs. They were ready to coast through the last week or two of classes and into the holiday break without thinking any further about the underside of society.

I opened the classroom door and quietly walked in without saying a word. This behavior alerted them because I normally greet my classes with as much enthusiasm as a person who is not on methamphetamines or cocaine can muster. But that day I quietly walked to the front of the class and stood before them. By now, most of the students realized that class would be different that afternoon and ceased talking among themselves. Quickly they quieted down and expectantly looked in my direction.

I don't know how I looked to them, but it could not have been relaxed. I felt dirty and overwhelmed. I felt as though *I* were the one that had a week left to live and was somehow supposed to act as if nothing had changed.

I then realized that I had come to class without my books or notes on that hour's subject. I had previously planned to discuss world religions and society, one of my favorite topics, but I felt completely unprepared, both physically and emotionally. I don't know why I bothered to show up for class at all that day. Perhaps because I looked to the students to provide a stable and comforting environment after my unsettling phone call just minutes before.

I didn't know what I was going to say, but when I opened my mouth this is what came out: "Um ... I ... uh. I just got a phone call. I mean an e-mail and then a phone call ... um ... and in six days I am going to Florida to serve as a witness for the State of Florida when they kill a guy ... I mean I am going to Florida next week to watch an execu-tion. I just ... um ... I just don't know what to say or how to feel about this right now ... I am going to watch them kill a guy."

The students stared at me with various facial ex-pressions. One girl, who had been very vocal and opinion-ated throughout the class, softly laid her head on her desk, covered her eyes and began to cry. Another student, a young man, looked at me with amazement and awe, as if I had just won the lottery. Most students, however, just stared at me or quietly looked around at each other without say-ing a word. For once, and as a whole, I had their undivided attention.

I mumbled for about five minutes on how the whole situation occurred. I described the article I read on the news Web site and the letters I wrote and then forgot about. Then I described the surreal phone conversation that I'd had just ten minutes before coming to class. After that, I opened the floor to questions. There were many, and they weren't easy ones to answer.

Sometimes I like to pretend I'm smart. I imagine that I, the bright young university professor, have the whole world figured out. I look at other people's mistakes, and sometimes think to myself, "I'm glad I'm smarter than *that* guy." But then I do something really stupid. I mean incredibly stupid, and with such little foresight, that I seriously consider tattooing the word "IDIOT" on my face to assure that no one ever again mistakes me for an intelligent person. When a student asked me, "How do they execute people in Florida?" I knew that this was one of those times.

With his question, I instantly remembered seeing national headlines about two of Florida's recent executions that had not gone according to plan. Both incidents occurred in the Florida State Prison in Starke, where I would be going the following Thursday. On July 8, 1999, Allen "Tiny" Davis was electrocuted in a gruesome execution witnessed by a dozen observers. Davis, who weighed 350 pounds, had savagely murdered a mother and her two daughters during a burglary in their home. For his crime, he received the death penalty to be carried out in the electric chair.

When the day arrived, he was strapped into the electric chair and a leather mask was placed over his face. Davis immediately started screaming and he continued to do so as the executioner threw the switch that sent 2,300 volts of electricity through his skull. During the 45 second electrocution, blood began pouring out from beneath the leather mask onto his chest, in front of the sickened witnesses. In the end, his white shirt was covered in his own blood while his chest and body jerked with spasms.

That day the witnesses expected to view a quick and painless death by the electric chair. What they saw, instead, was a bloody spectacle. When the mask was taken off, Davis' face was contorted, bloody and burned into a shocked expression. Physicians present during the execution determined that Davis, who had high blood pressure, simply experienced a typical bloody nose during the procedure, and while it looked ghastly, they assured all present that this really had been quite a "normal" execution.

The other incident that made the national papers involved Pedro Medina, who was convicted of killing a schoolteacher in Florida in 1982. In March 1997, Medina sat in the electric chair in the Florida State Prison in Starke. After Medina had been strapped into the very old and worn-out device, the executioner threw a switch and sent several thousand volts of electricity through the man's head and out his leg. Medina clenched his fists and violently arched his back as the fatal current slammed through his brain.

Seconds later, with horrified onlookers and witnesses present, fire and smoke began shooting out of Medina's head as he continued to be electrocuted. His head and face were on fire. The room filled with smoke and several witnesses became sickened and nauseated at the smell of cooking human flesh.

After the execution, three physicians reported that Medina was killed instantly. They stated that he did not feel the flames and appeared to have no "physical response" to the fire that poured out of his leather mask. The lack of "physical response," they believed, meant that he was unconscious during the execution. However, opponents of the death penalty countered that Medina wasn't unconscious. Citing that electricity causes a person to lose control of his or her muscles, they claimed that the current instead paralyzed Medina. They maintained that the man was fully awake and could feel what was happening to him throughout most of the ordeal, including the flames that were burning his face and head.

After Medina's alarming and brutal death, one Florida politician publicly stated that Medina's botched execution was actually good for the state of Florida, adding that it would serve as a deterrent to others. Speaking before the media, this government representative warned murderers that they should not come to Florida since the state was experiencing problems with its electric chair and convicted killers might die a painful and fiery death.

The images of both these bungled executions flooded my mind when the student posed his question about Florida's method of execution. When I wrote that fateful letter to the State of Florida, it never occurred to me that I might be requesting to sit nearby and watch as a man is burned to death with electricity. I don't remember what I imagined would occur in the death chamber, but an electrocution was definitely *not* it.

Before I could answer the first young man, a visibly excited student inquired, "Well, if you decide not to do it, can I go in your place? Will you let them know that I am in your class and that I can go instead?" Confused, I asked the student why he would want go to an execution.

"I don't know ... I just think it would be cool to watch," he replied, shrugging his shoulders slightly. I told him that if I did not go to the execution, I would definitely *not* suggest his name, since he seemed to want to go only for a cheap thrill. He gave a disappointed sigh and asked no further questions during the class.

But why did I agree to go? Did I feel an obligation for some reason? Did I have a morbid curiosity just like the student? Or, was it more noble than that? And if it was, who was I trying to help? Would I be able to physically watch an execution? My own questions during that hour were tougher than those raised by the class, and I failed to answer them to my own satisfaction.

By the end of the 50-minute class period, I had made another decision. If the execution was by electrocution, I might still go to the prison and sit in the death chamber with the prisoner, but I didn't think I could actually watch the death. Certainly this would hinder my understanding of the event. But I really did not think I could watch someone's head catch on fire or blood pour from a man's face as his body convulsed with electricity.

However, if the death were to occur by lethal injection, I would watch the death sentence carried out and I would try to make sense of it as best I could. I would take the information that I learned and use it to help expand the knowledge of my students, who rely on me as a resource to explain human behavior.

When the possibility became a reality that day, I knew without a doubt that I did *not* want to watch an execution. I was afraid and felt sick. But I decided that I would force myself to go, regardless of my revulsion for the thought.

I had begun to see this upcoming hardship as a necessary learning experience. Despite the pain and anguish it would certainly cause me as a person, I began to consider it similar to a difficult college exam, or to being embarrassed during a physical examination by a doctor. Despite the frustration and fear that exams created for me in school, I learned vast amounts of information by studying for them. And the humiliating and uncomfortable physical exams that we are all subject to provide benefits to our long-term health. True, academic exams and physical exams are both unpleasant while they last, but the overall benefits certainly outweigh the costs. This is how I wanted to understand Edward Castro's execution.

I had decided that I would watch a man die as punishment for a horrible crime. The whole experience would probably make me physically sick, and might even scar me emotionally for the rest of my life. But I would still watch him being killed. A part of me was tormented with self-anger at my decision. On the other hand, I believed that as a social scientist, I had the responsibility to create and refine knowledge about the social world and the behaviors that drive us. It was my job to play the investigator into the nature and causes of violent criminal behavior.

I would go to the prison in Florida and I would watch a man being killed.

CHAPTER ELEVEN

Two hours later, I closed and locked my office door, and walked outside to meet my wife. Camille and I shared a car; she and the kids were waiting to drive me home. I didn't know how she would respond to the news I had for her, but I thought that if I was careful and let her know gently and slowly, and in the right context, she would understand and be supportive of me.

With that in mind, I smiled as I approached her waiting in the parking lot, in the same minivan I'd used for the recent goose-hunting trip with my son. As I was getting into the car, I noticed that the kids were asleep inside. Camille greeted me in her usual cheerful voice, "Hello there. How was your day?"

"OK, I guess," I replied flatly. "I am going to Florida next week to watch a guy be executed for murder. That is, if we can work it out financially. I will watch him be killed ... Is that OK with you?"

So much for being careful.

I had never had to tell my wife anything like this before, and it just fell out of my mouth. The shocked and disappointed look on her face told me that it hadn't come out *quite* the way that I had hoped.

"Please tell me you're kidding," she said cautiously.

"No, really. I got a call from them, actually it was an e-mail, and they asked me if I wanted to serve as an official witness for the State of Florida during the execution."

"You are not going to do it, are you?"

I replied as though watching an execution was the most natural thing in the world. "Of course I am! This is my career. This is important research; I *have* to do it. Why are you so upset?" I knew exactly why she was upset, but I thought that if I acted innocently enough she might just drop the issue and say something like, "OK, you can watch an execution, but you had better be home by Saturday because the Smiths are coming over for dinner." That's what I hoped she'd say.

Instead she blurted out, "Why do you think I'm upset?" The disbelief on her face made it clear that she thought I was acting like a lunatic. And I was. "You are going to watch a man die? You can't do this! I'm sorry, that is just wrong!"

I responded to Camille's anger by becoming defensive and defiantly raised the stakes; "I *am* going to do this. I went to college for years to do things like this. What, am I just supposed to say, 'No, I don't want to go?' "

"Yes! That's *exactly* what you should say! Tell them you can't do it. I don't care what your degree is; you didn't study *this* in college! You can't do this."

Defiance wasn't working so I tried a different approach. "Camille, I *have* to do this. I study what is wrong with people and what motivates them to kill and attack themselves and others. This is my job and you know it." I wanted her to think something cosmic in the universe was directing me and the decision was totally out of my hands.

"What about us? I can't live with a man who watched someone being killed! This won't go ever away." She wasn't yet crying, but she was getting close. Then she said the words that later would prove to be almost prophetic: "Besides, you can't deal with things like this. You know you can't handle death, what makes you think you can handle *this*?" The bottom line was that Camille was opposed to the death penalty and objected to her husband having anything to do with the killing of another person.

For the rest of the day, the argument continued. Camille tried appealing to my sense of compassion for the condemned man, my love for my family, my dedication to my religion, and every other argument she could think of. She was angry and hurt, but sensible. I countered her points like a Nazi, with the simple retort that watching an execution was my job. It was what I did, and if I didn't take this opportunity to better understand the death penalty and explain it to others, who would? I was defensive and overly sure of myself.

In my mind, I rationalized that professors and researchers often choose to look at the ugly side of the world in an effort to understand it and explain it to others. While I didn't always like the subjects I studied, I did always feel that the world was, in some small way, a better place for my having done the research.

Or maybe I was just making excuses to justify what I was about to do. It's hard to tell. There was probably a little bit of both going on that day. But I had made up my mind on the matter. I had decided that this was something I should do and I simply expected her support. I was feeling desperately vulnerable and scared of what I was going to see, and I didn't think I could do it *without* her support.

After another hour of sparring with my wife on the competing subjects of "right" and "wrong," we realized that we were at an impasse. I was going to go, and she was going to be angry and disappointed with me for it. I didn't know how long the painful stalemate would last, but I was beginning to have the feeling that by going to Florida I was taking an enormous gamble, without knowing what the payoff, or loss, would be.

CHAPTER TWELVE

I was determined to find out as soon as possible all the information that I could about not only the condemned killers, but also about executions in the state of Florida. By now it was Friday evening and I knew that the records offices at most police departments in Florida would be closed for the night, so the phone calls would have to wait until Monday.

My research until then would be limited to the Internet. I first went to the web page of the Florida Supreme Court. There I quickly found information on the state's execution methods. I learned that due to the problems with Florida's electric chair, and the "botched" executions that resulted, inmates who were scheduled to die were given the choice of death by electrocution or death by lethal injection. This new policy began Jan. 1, 2000, and I took some comfort in believing that both prisoners would probably select lethal injection.

In fact, it seemed probable that no inmate in Florida would *ever* choose the electric chair. Essentially, the inmate could choose a death with the possibility of being painfully burned alive, or he could choose what I thought was a painless one, where the inmate simply fell asleep. Like others, I held the common belief that with lethal injection the patient is given a shot after which they go to sleep and simply never wake up. We are led to believe that the patient does not feel pain and is not aware that his heart stops beating. He simply dies.

From its beginning, the electric chair has been known to result not in immediate and humane executions, but often in deaths that can only be called, for a lack of a better term, torturous. One of the earliest blundered electrocutions happened to be one of the very first uses of the electric chair. In 1903, the State of New York executed Frederick Van Wormer in the electric chair. Van Wormer was strapped into the chair and the customary voltage was applied to his head causing violent shaking and the usual smell of burning human flesh.

When the electrocution was complete, workers placed Van Wormer's corpse on an autopsy table and went home for the day. After a short while, the "corpse" began to move. Physicians examined Van Wormer and quickly realized he was still alive. The man had survived the unbelievable ordeal and was still breathing. Authorities concluded that Van Wormer, because he was still alive, had not yet fully received the punishment that was intended for him, death, and so the executioner was called back to the prison to electrocute the man again. However, Van Wormer died before he could be strapped into the electric chair for another cycle of current.

Of course, this was nearly 100 years ago, and one should expect problems with any technology still in its infancy. But in the case of the electric chair, the technology has not noticeably improved over the past century. Many instances of electric chair malfunctions have been documented.

One such case occurred in Alabama in 1983. Inmate John L. Evans was scheduled to die by electrocution at the State Prison on April 12 at 8:30 p.m. In preparation for the electrocution, the guards strapped Evans into the chair and attached two electrodes to his body, one at his calf and the other in the form of a metal cap over his head. The man's face was next covered with a leather mask.

At the appointed moment, the executioner threw the switch, sending nearly 2000 volts of electricity into Evans' brain. Fire and smoke soon began shooting out of the electrode attached to his leg as Evans slammed against the chair and the leather straps holding him down. His hands clenched into impossibly tight fists as sparks flew and thick smoke poured out of the dark leather mask covering Evans' face. Witnesses could smell him cooking, as odors of burning human flesh and smoldering clothing filled the observation room.

At the end of the ordeal, two physicians examined Evans. To the horror of everyone in the room, probably including Evans himself, the doctors determined that the man was still alive. Before a room full of witnesses, electrical current ripped through John L. Evans, raising his body temperature to unthinkable levels. His skin, flesh and blood had begun to cook and unbelievably, the poor man was still alive.

Officials discovered that the electrode on Evans' leg had fallen off, interrupting the complete circuit of electricity through his body, which prevented his receiving voltage high enough to kill him. It was reattached and the leather straps and equipment were rechecked so that Evans' execution could continue.

When all the personnel were again in position, another electric current slammed into Evans' already severely burned body. For an additional 30 seconds, thousands of volts of electricity fried Evans to death in front of a room full of observers. His head and body began to smoke and discolor from the extreme heat of the electricity. Those in attendance reported that the smell of Evans' electrocution was overpowering and rancid, making many of the observers physically sick.

After the second electrocution, attending physicians again examined Evans. However, instead of pronouncing him dead, the doctors quickly realized that Evans was still alive. He had been burned alive twice in the space of several minutes and had endured it all. The man's internal organs were cooked inside him and somehow he had survived.

The witnesses and prison officials both stared in disbelief at the impossible sight before them. Either Evans' will to live was beyond that of any ordinary human being, or the electric chair was malfunctioning. And if it was malfunctioning, was it capable of delivering a shock sufficient enough to kill the man?

Prison officials were now presented with an unthinkable dilemma. In theory, Evans should have been killed instantly when the electricity shot through his head and heart. Since the heart is a muscle, it should have stopped beating after the tremendous amount of voltage had passed through it. But that hadn't happened, reinforcing the possibility that Alabama's electric chair might be malfunctioning. If so, further electrocution of Evans would continue to scorch and burn him, but he would not die from the shock of the electric current.

Prison officials were now faced with several options. They could remove Evans from the electric chair, which he had now survived twice, and treat his severe injuries in a burn center until the problem with the chair could be identified and corrected. This might take minutes, hours, or days. In the meantime, Evans would live in constant agonizing pain waiting for the moment when he would be strapped into the chair and electrocuted again.

Alternatively, prison officials could remove Evans from the chair, place him on the hospital gurney, already waiting for his corpse, and simply let him die. This is, after all, the intent of an execution. The inmate is to die from the injuries he sustains at the hands of the state. And with the extensive burns and the damage to his internal organs, Evans would not survive for long. With this option, officials could simply leave him alone on a bed and examine him periodically to see if he had died yet.

The final option they had available to them was to leave John Evans hooked up to the poorly-working electric chair, turn it on again and again, and continue electrocuting him until he finally died. But how many times would he, and his family and the witnesses, have to go through the process? The horrible answer to the question was, "As many times as it takes to kill him."

One would expect that he would only be electrocuted one or two more times at the most, three or four more times at the *very* most. Really, he *would* be dead by that point. Maybe five more electrocutions, but certainly no more than six or seven. He just could not live that long ... that is, it was *more than likely* that he could not live that long. But then again, he did survive two electrocutions that raised his body temperature to what was estimated to be over 250 degrees Fahrenheit. Maybe he would survive more.

Officials again electrocuted John L. Evans for another 30 seconds. By the time this third electrocution began, over ten minutes had passed since he was first electrocuted "to death." After the third electrocution, physicians placed a stethoscope against the burning hot skin of his chest and listened for a heartbeat. After several minutes, they determined that Evans had finally died. The first electrocution of John Evans began at 8:30 p.m., but he was not pronounced dead until 8:44 p.m., April 12, 1983; the execution of John L. Evans by the State of Alabama was finally completed. His torturous death in the Alabama electric chair took 14 minutes.

One could only hope that this would be an unusual case in modern America. Freak accidents do happen, after all. They happen everywhere, including in the home, at work and in school. Even proponents of the electric chair admit that accidents occasionally happen, even during executions. But they are quick to maintain that such accidents are very rare.

However, the facts simply don't support that argument. In reality, there are many cases of executions in the electric chair that can only be described as barbaric. Eventually, even advocates of the electric chair must begin to question that method of execution. If repeated electrocutions of prisoners, flaming skin and clothing, and the violent explosion of internal organs are common, then the electric chair must be a primitive, cruel, and horrible machine that tortures prisoners to death. In 2001, the state of Georgia, which has long been a proponent of capital punishment, adopted that same position.

In October 2001, after Georgia had executed a total of 441 people, the state's Supreme Court ruled that the electric chair was unconstitutional, citing that it constituted cruel and unusual punishment. In the ruling, the Justices wrote, "with its specter of excruciating pain and its certainty of cooked brains and blistered bodies, it violates the prohibition against cruel and unusual punishment."

The debate about the appropriateness or humanity of using the electric chair has influenced most states in the United States to begin using lethal injection as an alternative to electrocutions. In addition to Florida and Georgia, at least five other states have added execution by lethal injection as a choice for condemned prisoners over the last decade. This trend is the direct result of the miserable way in which electrocuted prisoners normally die. It is also in response to numerous articles and studies that have shown that "botched executions" in electric chairs are actually very common occurrences. Alabama, Arizona, Kentucky, Tennessee, and Texas have gone from using only the electric chair to either using lethal injection exclusively or giving prisoners a choice between the two. On July 1, 2002, Alabama switched to lethal injection only and Nebraska gained the distinction of becoming the only state in the union that still executes condemned killers solely by the use of the electric chair.

Ironically, there are some cases in which the prisoner actually *chooses* the electric chair over lethal injection, exactly *because* of how violent and horrible the execution is. In doing this, the inmate attempts to make a statement to our society that *all* executions are cruel and unusual and are, therefore, unconstitutional. A recent example of this was in September 2001, when death row inmate John W. Byrd chose the electric chair over lethal injection to end his life.

Byrd was sentenced to die in the state of Ohio for his part in the 1983 stabbing death of Cincinnati convenience store clerk, Monte Tewksbury. Byrd and an accomplice, John Brewer, used a knife to commit armed robbery. By his own admission, after securing the cash from the store register, John Brewer stabbed Tewksbury to death. In separate trials, both Byrd and Brewer were found guilty of murder. Brewer, the man who actually stabbed Tewksbury, was sentenced to life imprisonment. However, after the jury deliberated on the case of John W. Byrd, the accomplice who didn't commit the actual murder, they sentenced him to death. Byrd strongly maintained his innocence through the trial and his time on death row, and Brewer, again, maintained that he, not Byrd, had stabbed the clerk.

As in other states, Ohio has a provision in its death sentence law that allows death row inmates to choose between lethal injection and the electric chair. That state hadn't used the electric chair since 1963, and Byrd chose it because he knew that Ohio didn't want to use that method ever again. State officials tried to convince Byrd to choose lethal injection, arguing that that method was more humane and less painful. But Byrd refused and held that if the state of Ohio was going to execute an innocent man, he was going to make it as difficult for it as possible and force it to electrocute him.

Facing this unusual situation, an Ohio prison official announced that the state refused to subject prison guards and other employees to the brutality of an electrocution. He added that they would rather commute Byrd's sentence to life in prison than to perform something as disturbing as electrocution.

In reality, Byrd didn't want to die at all, especially by electrocution. He knew he didn't actually kill the convenience store clerk and was counting on the fact that the citizens of Ohio would not allow him, a man who didn't kill anyone, to be executed in such a gruesome manner. The state of Ohio granted a stay of execution, to determine how to resolve the matter, and for a time, Byrd got what he wanted: a reprieve.

During Byrd's stay of execution, the Ohio State Legislature banned the use of the electric chair in executions. Thus, lethal injection remained as the sole method of administering the death penalty, and Byrd was then rescheduled to die by lethal injection. Byrd then argued that even though lethal injection is less painful for the prisoner, it was still unconstitutional in his case. He claimed that since he was innocent of the murder committed during the crime, any execution would violate his civil rights. The United States Supreme Court refused to hear his case and Byrd was executed, by lethal injection, on Feb. 19, 2002.

As I searched the Internet that evening, I discovered the protocol for execution by lethal injection in the State of Florida. It was detailed in the Florida State Supreme Court case of Sims vs. Florida, which was handed down on March 3, 2000. Although the protocol for death by lethal injection is slightly different from state to state, most follow the same general procedure used by the State of Florida. The decision contained the following description:

"On the morning of the execution, the inmate will receive a physical examination [On the surface, this is one of the more ironic parts of the execution: ensuring that the prisoner is healthy before they are executed. This is done to verify that the prisoner has been well-treated during his or her time on death row], be given a Valium if necessary to calm anxiety, and will receive his or her last meal. Next, the inmate will be taken to the execution room where he will be strapped to a gurney and placed on a heart monitor. The inmate will then be injected with two IVs containing saline solution. He will then be escorted into the execution chamber where the witnesses will be able to view the execution. [While the court ruling doesn't state it, at this point the inmate is given an opportunity to make a final statement, or "last words" to the witnesses]. While the inmate is being prepared, a pharmacist will prepare the lethal substances. In all, a total of eight syringes will be used; each of which will be injected in a consecutive order into the IV tube attached to the inmate. The first two syringes will contain 'no less than' two grams of sodium pentothal, an ultra-short acting barbiturate which renders the inmate unconscious. The third syringe will contain a saline solution to act as a flushing agent. The fourth and fifth syringes will contain no less than fifty milligrams of pancuronium bromide, which paralyzes the muscles. The sixth syringe will contain saline, again as a flushing agent. Finally, the seventh and eighth syringes will contain no less than one hundred and fifty milliequivalents of potassium chloride, which stops the heart from beating. Each syringe will be numbered to ensure that they are injected into the IV tube in the proper order. A physician will stand behind the executioner while the chemicals are being injected. The physician's assistant will also observe the execution and will certify the inmate's death upon completion of the execution. These procedures were created with the purpose of accomplish[ing] our mission with humane dignity [while] carrying out the court's sentence."

The verdict continues, "On the issue of dosage, a[n] ... expert admitted that only one milligram per kilogram of body weight is necessary to induce unconsciousness, and that a barbiturate coma is induced at five milligrams per kilogram of body weight. Thus, two grams of sodium pentothal (i.e., 2000 milligrams) is a lethal dose and certain to cause rapid loss of consciousness (i.e., within 30 seconds of injection). The expert further stated that muscle paralysis occurs at 0.1 milligram of pancuronium bromide per kilogram of body weight. Thus, fifty milligrams of pancuronium bromide far exceeds the amount necessary to achieve complete muscle paralysis. Finally, the expert admitted that 150 to 250 milliequivalents of potassium chloride would cause the heart to stop if injected quickly into the inmate and that an IV push would qualify as 'quickly.' "

This information comforted me a bit. I thought I might just be able to watch such a procedure. In reading the description in the Supreme Court ruling that evening, it sounded to me like execution by lethal injection was clinical, painless and nonviolent. It had been designed with so many back-up measures in place that there seemed to be no possibility that a prisoner might live through it. To the milliliter, the procedure I was to see next week would be carried out according to plan.

However, as I dug further, I became anxious once again. It seems the physiology of every person, including prison inmates, varies. Not all veins are of equal size and not all metabolisms function at the same rate. In theory, the poisons should kill the person instantly, but even getting the poison into the condemned is occasionally difficult.

Six months before I would step into the exact the same room, just such a situation occurred in the Florida State Prison. On June 8, 2000, Bennie Demps, a convicted murderer who had been on death row for over 22 years, was scheduled to die by lethal injection. Demps was strapped onto the gurney and medical technicians began probing his arms for veins in which to insert one needle each. Thirty-three minutes later, prison employees wheeled the man into the death chamber.

Demps made his final, angry comments before the witnesses, "They butchered me back there! I was in a lot of pain. They cut me in the groin. They cut me in the leg. I was bleeding profusely ... This is not an execution ... this is a murder!"

Medical technicians often have difficulty finding a suitable vein in which to insert the needle and tubing. That day they easily found a vein in one of Demps' arms, but the second arm proved more challenging. In their attempt to locate a second vein, the technicians cut into Demps' flesh in several different places. After cutting Demps repeatedly for half an hour, officials finally gave up and executed him with only one needle. Once the chemicals entered the man's bloodstream, he died fairly quickly. But if one believes his final statements, Demps suffered a great deal of pain, for a significant length of time, before the execution was carried out. After reading the state of Florida's description of the procedure, I would not have suspected that trauma in lethal injections was possible. Death by lethal injection sounded relatively controlled, and thus uneventful.

Thinking of the botched electric chair executions I had read a great deal about, I became curious to see how the state of Florida described *that* method of execution. I found the following description of the protocol from the Committee on Criminal Justice of the Florida State Senate:

"Executions [by electrocution] are performed at Florida State Prison in Starke, Florida. The following is a partial description of Florida's protocol on execution by electrocution.

"Prior to each execution, the execution equipment is tested. Additionally, testing of the execution equipment is performed a minimum of eight times each year. A "mock" execution is performed prior to each actual execution.

"Florida employs a single executioner. The executioner must exhibit a willingness to participate and must uphold the confidentiality of the execution proceedings. To select an executioner, the position is originally advertised in newspapers. Applications are taken and evaluated. Applicants are interviewed (but are not given a psychological evaluation). The Florida Department of Corrections does not report who conducts these interviews or evaluations or who selects the executioner, nor does the department report whether the executioner serves only for a single execution or serves until he resigns or is replaced. The executioner is compensated [meaning the executioner is paid].

"The execution team consists of administrative, maintenance, security, and medical staff who are selected by the superintendent of Florida State Prison. The superintendent is in charge of the team. The execution team members are not compensated for their services. Service on the team is voluntary for all members except for the superintendent and the medical executive director ...

"Staff at Florida State Prison supervises the shaving of the crown of the condemned offender's head and the offender's right leg from the knee to the ankle.

"Official witnesses, who have reported to Florida State Prison's Administration Building, are greeted by two designated Department of Corrections' staff and, as a group, are escorted by the designated staff to the main entrance of Florida State Prison, cleared by security, and escorted to the staff dining room where they remain until escorted to the witness room of the execution chamber by the designated escort staff.

"The offender is escorted to the shower area. Following the shower, the offender is returned to his assigned cell and issued underwear, a pair of trousers, a dress shirt or blouse (as appropriate) and socks. The offender wears no shoes. A suit coat is not worn by the offender during the execution but is placed on the offender's body after the execution proceedings.

"At the direction of the superintendent, all calls are forwarded to the execution chamber from the Governor's office through a switchboard extension. Should institutional telephone lines fail at any time during the process, the switchboard operator immediately advises the Command Center, which is located within hearing range of the switchboard operator. Telephones in the execution chamber are checked. Staff also ensures that a fully-charged cellular telephone is in the execution chamber. Sample telephone calls are placed to each telephone to ensure proper operation. The public address system is also checked to ensure its proper operation.

"A saturated saline solution is mixed and two natural sea sponges are placed in the solution [it is suspected that the reason Medina caught on fire during his execution, described earlier, is because a *synthetic* sponge was used].

"Staff establishes telephone communication with the Governor's office on behalf of the superintendent. This phone line remains open during the entire execution proceeding.

"Staff verifies that water on X-wing is turned off.

" ... Staff ensures that a salt-free, hypoallergenic, electrically-conducive gel is applied to the crown of the offender's shaven head and the calf of the offender's right leg in a total application of approximately 4 ounces.

"Just prior to the execution, the superintendent reads the death warrant to the offender and the offender is allowed to make a last statement.

"Official witnesses are secured in the witness room of the execution chamber by two designated Department of Corrections' escort staff. The same procedure is followed with the media witnesses. The witness room of the execution chamber is secured. The execution chamber is secured.

"Staff applies restraints to the offender for escort into the execution chamber. Prior to the offender being escorted, security arrangements have been made for his movement from his Q-wing cell to the execution chamber in compliance with a schedule set by the superintendent. At the offender's request and subject to the approval of the superintendent or assistant superintendent, the chaplain may accompany the offender to the execution chamber. The time is recorded when the offender enters the chamber.

"The offender enters the execution chamber and is placed in the electric chair. The chair is constructed of oak and is set on a rubber matting and bolted to a concrete floor. Lap, chest, arm, and forearm straps are secured. When the straps are secured, the restraints are removed and ankle straps are secured. A leg piece (anklet) is laced to the offender's right calf and a sponge and electrode is attached. Staff ensures that the sponge covers all areas of the electrode to prevent any contact of the electrode with the offender's skin, and also ensures that the sponge is sufficiently wet (slightly dripping). The headpiece is secured. The headgear consists of a metal headpiece covered with a leather hood, which conceals the offender's face. The metal part of the headpiece consists of a copper wire mesh screen to which the electrode is brazened. A wet sponge is placed between the electrode and the offender's scalp.

Excess saline solution from the sponge is dried with a clean towel. During the execution, two Department of Corrections' staff members are posted in the execution chamber to ensure that the offender is seated and that the electrocution equipment is properly connected.

"A staff member then proceeds to the outside open telephone line to inquire of any possible stays of execution. If there are no stays, the execution proceeds.

"The safety switch is closed. The circuit breaker is engaged. The execution control panel is activated. The executioner is signaled either verbally or by gesture to engage the execution switch and the automatic cycle begins. While the automatic cycle has five cycles, only three cycles are used.

"The automatic cycle begins with the programmed 2,300 volts (9.5 amps) for eight seconds, followed by 1,000 volts (4 amps) for 22 seconds, followed by 2,300 volts (9.5 amps) for eight seconds. When the cycle is complete, the electrician indicates that the current is off. Equipment is disconnected. The manual circuit behind the chair is disengaged. The safety switch is opened. The time in which the execution switch is disengaged is recorded.

"Two minutes after the electrical current ceases, the physician examines the offender's body for vital signs. The physician pronounces the offender's death and the time of death. The estimated average length of time that elapses from the time the offender is restrained to the time that death is determined is 10 minutes. The physician signs the death certificate and the physician and physician's assistant ensure that the proper documents are recorded. If the offender is not pronounced dead [the procedure does not address if the person is "still alive", only if they are "not pronounced dead"], the execution cycle is then ordered to be repeated.

"The Governor is notified via the open phone line that the sentence has been carried out and that the offender has been pronounced dead. There is another announcement to the official witnesses and the media that the sentence has been carried out. Then, the witnesses and media are directed to exit the witness room."

This, too, sounded equally clinical to me. The writing made very little mention of what happens if the prisoner doesn't actually *die* from the electrocution. I became even more concerned about what to expect the following Thursday afternoon, since I began to suspect that even "typical" executions could be gruesome.

CHAPTER THIRTEEN

On the day of the first scheduled execution, Dec. 7, 2000, the clock-radio next to my bed exploded to life at 2:00 in the morning. I had set the alarm to go off at that insane hour to allow me time to make the three-hour drive to the Minneapolis/St. Paul airport and catch the first flight out that morning to Jacksonville, Florida.

As I stumbled out of bed, I glanced out the window at the familiar haze and falling snow of a typical Minnesota winter night. The forecast on the evening news the night before had warned that up to two feet of snow could fall the next day, and it appeared to be starting already. I expected the three-hour, pre-dawn drive through the small farming towns to be less monotonous and more frightening than usual.

I was thinking about Edward Castro the instant my alarm sounded, and then for every oppressive second after that while I got ready. My mouth felt dry, my heart was racing, and my thoughts seemed more scattered than usual. I shuffled around my dark and silent house, showering, forcing down a light breakfast, and preparing to view death. My bags were waiting in the idling minivan outside and it was finally time to say goodbye to my family.

I gently opened the door to the bedroom of my baby boy, Jonathan. I smiled to see that he was sleeping peacefully. I stroked his soft hair with my fingertips before leaving to check on his brothers. In the next room, Quinn and Nathaniel shared a bed. I bent over them and listened carefully to make sure both were breathing. Then I kissed each one on the top of the head and whispered how much I loved them.

As I climbed the stairs back to my bedroom, I wondered to myself, "If anyone were ever to kill one of my children, would I want that killer to be executed?" With the luxury of having my children alive and well, I thought "No, that wouldn't solve anything."

I gently pushed open the door of our bedroom and heard my wife snoring softly. I gently touched her blond hair and she startled awake, looking at the clock. "What are you doing?" she mumbled in a groggy voice that I had learned to understand over the last seven years.

"I have to go," I told her.

Without looking at me, she rolled over and said, a little more clearly this time, "Be careful and come home safely, OK?" I promised her I would, kissed her on the back of the head, and left the house, out into the freezing snowstorm.

Inside the van, I adjusted the heating controls and paused for a second, looking at the front of my pink house. Pink. I hated the color of the house. After moving in months earlier, I found an extra gallon of the paint in the basement and discovered that this disgusting color of my house was not actually called "pink." The label on the can identified the color as "Pottery." I guess the manufacturer though that name would sell better than "Pepto-Bismal-Pink." At times, the color of my house embarrassed me, but at that moment I sat and thought how perfect my life was. The pink paint didn't bother me one bit.

Not remembering if I prayed before I left the house, I did so in the van and then pulled out onto the deserted, snow-covered street. Several boring hours later, I parked in the Minneapolis/St. Paul airport, found my terminal, and waited for the plane's departure. Other passengers sat around me anxiously smiling and drinking ridiculously expensive designer coffee from a vendor on the concourse.

Some talked excitedly about leaving the Minnesota snow-storm for the sandy beaches of Florida. I didn't feel that way.

A small group of fellow passengers stood nearby, debating the presidential election battle still being fought. They argued back and forth whether George W. Bush or Al Gore had actually won the election. My less-vocal traveling companions had their noses buried in newspapers that kept the world up-to-date on the latest court ruling, vote count, and accusation of improper election procedure. While the world looked to that southern state to see who would be the next President of the United States, my mind was on an entirely different Florida matter.

When the gate agent announced my row number, I boarded the plane and took my seat by the window. I always request a window seat because if we crash, I will have a terrific view of my impending death. My fear of flying leads me to believe that each time a plane takes off with me in it, it is going to crash. I certainly know how unlikely a person is to be killed in a commercial plane wreck, but it does happens periodically, and the thought of it still terrifies me every time I fly.

I read somewhere that the most dangerous time for a plane is during the take off. The article said that most wrecks and accidents occur during the first several minutes of the flight. So I have trained myself to sleep for exactly 20 minutes after buckling up in an aircraft. I am not sure how I accomplished this feat, but it feels like a self-induced hypnosis. It washes over me like a wet, black shroud and then clears up at around 20,000 feet. I have never died in a commercial airplane accident and I attribute it to my self-hypnosis trick.

But that morning my heart rate was so high and I was so nervous and tense that I knew I could not count on sleeping to escape my phobia of flying. I couldn't stop thinking about death, in general, and more specifically, executions. It would have taken a strong shot of Valium, and I wished I'd had one, to get me slumbering. Unfortunately, I was not going to slip into unconsciousness through that particular take off.

To distract myself from our imminent departure, and possible crash, I took out one of the books I had brought to make the long flight pass more quickly. From the several choices in my carry-on bag, I selected the latest novel by Kurt Vonnegut. *God Bless You, Dr. Kevorkian* was the only book by this great author that I had not yet read, and so I didn't bother to find out what the story was before I checked it out at the library.

With the plane quickly gaining speed down the runway, I opened the cover to relax with some of Vonnegut's ridiculous wit. I quickly discovered that the entire story was set in the death chamber at Texas State Prison, under the watchful eye of Dr. Jack Kevorkian. I didn't know that Vonnegut wrote about death chambers, and I was not expecting one of his books to be on this subject. To put it mildly, I was shocked at this coincidence and immediately interpreted it as a bad sign.

A disturbing rush of anger, fear, and hopelessness filled me and I considered crying out loud. My hands shook visibly and I punched my fists into my legs in anger. I wanted to stop everything and start over. I felt myself slipping toward something unknown and each life-giving breath I took confused me further. I didn't understand this thing called "life," but I clung to it, breathed it, loved it, and was afraid of losing it. Yet I was traveling that morning to watch another man's life being taken away from him.

At last I knew.

In that moment, I had finally decided that it was wrong to kill another human being, even a murderer. I had just made up my mind, yet I couldn't stop myself from going through with the execution. Surprisingly, I felt compelled to watch. The part of me that earlier didn't want to see the killing was quickly vanishing. What remained was an empty shell that would walk into an execution chamber seven hours later and witness a man being killed. At that moment on the airplane, I believed I knew what it must feel like for Robert Ruger and Edward Castro, the two men who were about to die. I felt part of me was dying, too.

With the decision that I could take part in an execution, despite now clearly believing it to be morally wrong, I had changed in some way. The "me" that existed moments ago, before I fully decided to go through with the execution, to actually take part in it, had just been laid to rest. In a way, I had just killed myself.

My fit of panic and self-detachment, as I departed from the Minneapolis/St. Paul airport that morning, was the first glimpse of the extreme psychological toll the execution would take on me later that evening. The execution was not to be just Edward Castro's. It was mine, too.

It would be our execution—together.

Jacksonville

Starke

Ocala

Euwella

St. Petersburg

Diagram by Marc Kendig

EDWARD CASTRO

DEATH HOUSE

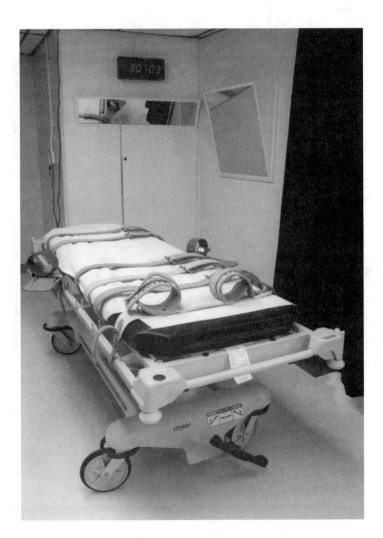

DEATH CHAMBER GURNEY

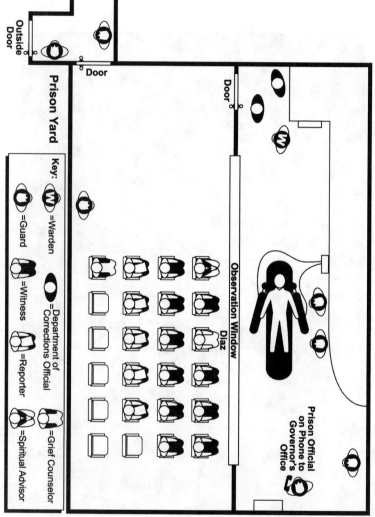

Diagram by Marc Kendig

DEATH CHAMBER

CHAPTER FOURTEEN

Thanks, once again, to my self-hypnosis, I arrived in Florida physically intact. I picked up my one piece of luggage and headed outside to catch the shuttle bus for the off-site rental car agency where I had a reservation. When I left Minnesota several hours before, I had been in the middle of a blizzard with temperatures near zero. But now, as I stepped out of the artificially-cooled airport in Jacksonville, I was nearly blinded by the intense sun. I quickly became uncomfortable wearing my heavy, winter coat in the 80-degree weather.

I shed the jacket and waited on the curb with another traveler who had just arrived in Jacksonville. The middle-aged man, well over six feet tall, was covered with gaudy jewelry that looked to be worth more money than I earned in a year. He also wore a black leather coat emblazoned with the logo of the Jacksonville Jaguars, which I recognized as the newly established professional football team from the area. To complete the look, he also had on a Jacksonville Jaguars hat, a Jacksonville Jaguars watch, and he carried a black leather Jacksonville Jaguars briefcase. He looked like he was financially well-off and wanted others to know it.

When the shuttle bus arrived, I boarded right behind the walking advertisement for the Jacksonville Jaguars. I looked around the bus and saw that he and I were the only two passengers. To break the silence, I said to him "Let me guess—you work for the Chicago Bears."

He threw back his head and let out one of those phony, business-deal-golf-course-type laughs, which made me embarrassed for him. "No," he replied, "my son plays football for the Jaguars and I'm down here trying to sign a deal for him for the last few games of the season."

I didn't really have a response to that. "Oh, I see," I said, as intelligently as possible.

"What sort of business are you in?" he asked me, in a tone of voice that implied that whatever I was doing in Jacksonville was not nearly as important as what he was doing.

"Research and behavioral science," I replied. He did a poor job of sounding impressed, so I elaborated, "I'm a university professor and I research violent criminal behavior and social problems like suicide, drug use, gangs, juvenile crime, and murder."

That seemed to get his attention. "Do you work down here in Jacksonville?" he asked me.

"No, I live in Minnesota," I told him casually. "I'm just here for a few days to watch a man being executed for murder."

Both he and the bus driver, who I didn't know was listening, quickly looked up at me to see if I was kidding. Then it was his turn to give a weak response, sort of like the one I had given him moments before. "Wow," he said, and he followed his insightful comment with silence all the way to the rental car agency.

When the bus stopped, he and I picked up our suitcases at the same time and were about to pass through the doors. Just to be a further jerk, I reached into the pocket of my pants and pulled out a dollar bill that I had previously taken from my wallet. I didn't know if the conspicuously rich guy was planning to tip the bus driver or not, but I thought it would be fun to test him. People who flaunted their wealth tended to irritate me, anyway, and I was not in a very good mood that day. As I passed the driver, who was still sitting in his chair, I tipped him the dollar, making sure the other guy could see me do it. The man's face flashed embarrassment for a split-second, and he had to set down his luggage once again and remove his wallet from the Jacksonville Jaguars briefcase, in order to give the driver a dollar that he was obviously not planning on giving him before.

I left the bus, picked up the rental car, and headed out of town. On the cheap rental car stereo I found a radio station playing a Cheap Trick song. I cranked the volume up much too loud and headed south for the 90-mile drive to Starke.

Along the way, I passed a work crew, all dressed in bright orange clothing, on the side of the road. Some of the men appeared to be picking up trash while others were engaged in some work off to the side of a utility truck. Near the back of their truck was a sign announcing "Prison Inmates Working." I had seen this type of operation before in other states, and I think it's a very good idea. Requiring inmates to work forces those who have harmed society to improve it in some way. Work programs also teach prisoners how to labor and hold down a job, important skills to have if we hope to rehabilitate them and integrate them back into society.

But on that particular day, the sight of this prison crew reminded me of the reason I came to Florida. I felt guilty for listening to the radio and enjoying the drive. I turned the music off and drove in silence. In my mind, I formulated questions that I hoped someone down in Starke could answer.

Arriving at my destination, I found Starke to be a small, but inviting, town. I pulled into the first motel with a restaurant attached to it, and went inside to check in. The woman at the counter was making small talk as she typed in my information on the computer. She asked for my car's license plate number, and I made one up because I was too exhausted to go back outside and look. I nearly made it through the check-in process without "the question," but at the end she asked, "So what brings you to Starke?" Her tone indicated an equal mixture of friendliness and curiosity.

"I am down here to visit the prison," I vaguely replied.

"Yeah, I thought so," she told me, "that's the only reason people ever come to Starke." She handed me the room key adding, "OK, there you go. Enjoy your visit!"

"Thank you, I will try," I sincerely replied.

I unlocked the door to my room and began my usual motel-room ritual. First, I turn on the light and while still standing near the open front door, I open the shades completely. This allows me to see outside and others to see inside, so they can call the police if they see me being attacked. Next I check in the bathroom, to make sure there are no lunatics waiting in there to kill me. After that, I look under the bed. If the bed happens to be one of those that sits on a box-like pedestal, instead of a traditional frame, I always lift up the mattress and look inside of the box. A couple years earlier I began adding this particular step to my motel routine, after hearing a story where a motel maid found a dead body in one of those things.

I found no dead bodies under the bead or lunatics in my room, so I locked the door, closed the shade, and turned up the air conditioning to high. Then I called the prison to let them know that I had arrived safely, which they had asked me to do. I asked the receptionist to connect me to Ms. Harper, the woman I had talked with six days earlier when the whole mess started. In just a few seconds, she was on the line, "Hello, Dr. Diaz, are you in Starke?"

"Yes, ma'am," I confirmed. "I just checked into my motel."

She asked, "Can I get the hotel phone number and the room number where you're staying, please?" I thought she might be trying to flirt with me, but then she explained,

"We have to be able to get hold of you right away, in case the execution is canceled or anything else happens."

"So is Edward Castro's execution still on?" I asked.

"Yes it is, but the other man, Robert Ruger, the one who was scheduled for tomorrow? He was just granted a stay of execution. So there will just be the one execution. Remember to be here at 4:00, at the latest, and make sure you dress professionally, OK?"

I assured Ms. Harper that I would do exactly what was expected of me and then hung up the phone. The week before, when I had made my airline reservations, I scheduled Saturday as my departure date. Ruger's execution had been scheduled for Friday, and I might have watched it, had Castro's death been delayed or his sentence commuted to life in prison. Now that Ruger's execution was postponed and Castro's was moving forward, I would be stuck alone and 2000 miles from home, the day after I had just watched a man being killed.

For a moment I considered calling the airline. I thought about using the old "the second execution has been postponed" excuse, in order to change my departure date to Friday without incurring a penalty. But I decided against it, thinking that I might actually need the extra time to collect my thoughts, before I allowed my family to see me again.

CHAPTER FIFTEEN

By the time I finished talking with Ms. Harper, it was about 2:00 in the afternoon. I grabbed my wallet and headed down to the Denny's, conveniently attached to the motel, for a little "pre-execution" lunch.

I learned from the hostess who seated me, that it would take me about ten minutes to drive from the motel to the prison. Apparently she had made the trip before, and I wondered why.

Only two other tables inside the dining room were occupied at that off-peak hour. One of them held four women, who looked to me like if you added up all their ages, you might get a sum of around 350. They had finished eating their lunch and were sitting and talking about whatever old women sit in restaurants and talk quietly about.

In contrast, the other table was noisy and full of people. It was only about ten feet away from where I sat and it held two middle-aged women, a young woman in her early 20s, a teenage girl, another girl of junior-high school age, and two young children, both under the age of five.

The three adult women were eating ice cream, laughing, and talking loud enough for everyone else to hear. All three were large, in terms of height and weight, but couldn't accurately be described as obese. The kids, including the two older girls, kept getting up out of their chairs and walking to the cashier's counter, where they admired a display full of toys, cheap gifts and trinkets.

Every few minutes, one of the children would return to the table of adults and try some new tactic to get money from them to use at the toy and gift counter.

While waiting for my food and sipping my Diet Coke, I overheard the table of loud, ice-cream-eating women mention the word "execution," and my attention was now piqued. Since learning I would be coming to Florida, I decided I would try to interview the families of Edward Castro's victims. I wanted to hear their thoughts on the execution, and I wondered what they expected to get from watching Castro being killed. I also thought it would be important to talk to them again afterwards to find out if they had found a sense of peace or resolution after the killer's execution.

I had read that most families of victims feel only a further sense of loss after the execution of their loved one's killer. Generally they expect that "justice will be done" and that they will somehow feel better after watching the death of the killer. However, after the execution, most of them realize that the resolution that they seek comes from within themselves and from their own perspective, not from executing a killer. In other words, the death of a callous, cold-blooded killer can not pay for, in the minds of the victim's family, the brutal murder of their child, spouse, parent, or sibling. I wondered if this would be true for the execution I was about to watch.

I played with the lemon slice in my drink, wondering who the women sitting next to me were. They were discussing executions, but I wasn't yet comfortable approaching them. Instead, I listened to them talk loudly some more. For a brief moment I thought that perhaps it was wrong to listen to their conversation, but I quickly rationalized it by thinking that if it were a private conversation, they would not be announcing it out loud to a Denny's restaurant.

I couldn't hear everything the women were saying, but after a little time had passed, my ears kept catching the words "prison," "execution," and "Castro." About the time my food arrived, I left it, untouched on the table, and walked over to the group.

They stopped talking immediately and stared at me as I approached them. The three ladies were the only ones at the table; the children and young girls were at the gift counter again. The women glared at me with a look of distrust that I had never seen so strongly before in strangers.

"Excuse me," I said to them all collectively, "I heard you mention Castro and the execution and I thought I might come over to talk to you."

They did not say a single word. The women looked extremely guarded, afraid, and very nervous. I could see that I had made a mistake, but I didn't know who they were, and I didn't know how to recover from the awkward moment. I had the feeling that these were exactly the people I had hoped to talk with. I thought they might be the family of one of Castro's victim's, but I could easily see by their facial expressions that I was NOT welcome at their table.

I tried a different approach. "I'm Dr. Joseph Diaz," I started. "I am a professor of sociology and criminology and I am here in Florida researching the death penalty. I am going out to the prison in ... "

"Are you a reporter?" one of the older women interrupted, with a look of contempt.

"No, I'm a college professor. I was eating my lunch and I heard you mention Castro's name, so I thought I would come over."

"So you aren't a reporter or anything?"

"No, absolutely not," I assured her.

"Do you work for a newspaper," she persisted, this time with less hostility and more interest than before.

"No, I am a professor at a university in Minnesota. I do research and write studies, but no one reads the stuff that I write, and I am certainly not a reporter." I then showed the women my business card and my university identification.

As I stood in the middle of a Denny's restaurant, I thought I had made it through the hardest part of this difficult moment. But then the oldest of the three women asked a question that I was not at all ready to answer, "Well, do you support or oppose the death penalty?"

Her question reminded me of an article I had once read describing an incident that happened to a journalist covering the Middle East. He had been assigned to Tel Aviv to report on the escalating violence between the Jews and Palestinians in the area. One night, the reporter was walking near his hotel in an area thought to be relatively safe. As he was walking, a man came up behind him, put a gun to his head, cocked the hammer back and asked him one question, "Jew or Muslim?"

The reporter, who was neither a Muslim nor a Jew, went numb as his hands and body trembled with utter horror. He knew that he would only be allowed to answer with one word, either "Jew" or "Muslim." He briefly considered explaining that he was a neutral reporter but he feared that response might bring him instant death because the gunman may see him as an interloper involved in a conflict that was none of his affair. He had only a second to answer, and decided to say the first thing that came to his mind.

"Jew."

The gunman lowered his pistol, tucked it into his coat, turned and walked away. The reporter's answer bought him his life. But it could have just as easily meant death.

Like the reporter, I knew I had to give the right answer to her question, "Do you support or oppose the death penalty?" While my life was not on the line that afternoon at Denny's, my answer would determine if these women would talk to me further and perhaps bring clarity to my clouded mind. If this was the victim's family and I told them that I opposed the death penalty, they might tell me to get lost. On the other hand, they might be opposed to the death penalty and be angry if I said that I supported it.

As is always the best thing to do, I decided to tell them the truth. "I study criminal behavior for a living. I study it every single day and think about it all the time. I have read the reports. I have analyzed the data myself, and I am of the firm belief that the death penalty does not decrease the rate of violent crime. Further, very few, if any, murders are prevented by executing people, when we could just as easily keep the inmate in prison for life. So I think that because it not only doesn't help society, but, in fact, hurts society because there is the possibility of killing an innocent person, that the death penalty is a bad idea." It was clumsy and poorly-worded, but it was the truth. I was hardly breathing while I waited for their response.

The three women instantly relaxed. They leaned back in their chairs and smiled as if I was an old friend. Suddenly, they no longer looked at me with skepticism, as they had done just five seconds earlier. Instead, I felt a trust that approached the feeling of being with my family.

The mood change at the table prompted me to try another question. "Are you here for the Castro execution?" I ventured.

"No," replied the younger of the middle-aged women, "they were supposed to execute my husband tomorrow and we just found out that he was given a stay of execution." Her voice was amazingly calm and it left me dumbfounded. "Praise God. Praise the Lord for miracles," added one of the two older women, with what sounded like a great deal of sincerity.

I somehow found my breath and asked, "Do you mean you are Ruger's family?"

"Yep," one of them answered proudly, "he's my husband and this here is his daughter." She motioned to the young woman in the group that I had earlier guessed to be in her mid-20s.

"And he's my brother," announced the other middle-aged woman, now eager to join the conversation. "We all came down to see him. We just found out a minute ago that they ain't gonna kill him tomorrow, so we came in to have ice cream to celebrate it before we drive on home."

Executions had just become much more real to me.

Ruger's daughter then stood up from her chair and said, "look here," motioning for me to look at her tee shirt, which bore a large photo of the young woman standing with her father. In the picture, the girl towered over the much shorter Ruger, who wore his orange, death-row jumpsuit. Someone had obviously taken the photo of the two of them during a recent visit at the prison, and his daughter now proudly displayed this image of her with her father, a man on death row.

Since my phone conversation with Ms. Harper the Friday before, I had done some research on the two convicted killers and had uncovered one photo of Ruger. It had looked like every other mug shot I had seen, except for the orange jumpsuit used exclusively for death row inmates. In that photo, Ruger was not smiling. But he was broadly grinning in the image silk-screened onto on his daughter's shirt. He looked tiny in stature compared to his daughter, and I remembered reading that Ruger stood only 5 feet 4 inches tall and weighed around 140 pounds.

"He's not a very big guy, is he?" I asked.

The three women let out a good-natured laughed and Ruger's wife replied to me, "No, he's a little bitty old thing. But you should see when we visit him. He is surrounded by five guards watching every move he makes." Then she began to get angry, "I don't know if they think we are just gonna take him out of the prison or something. But they just stand there and stare at us like there's something gonna happen if they leave us all alone for just a minute."

"When they sentenced him to death they sentenced his family to death, too. No one ever thinks about his family, but we're suffering, too," Ruger's sister added. It sounded like a line that she had repeated many times before.

I watched his wife stare off at the wall, as her sister-in-law said these words. I remembered reading that Robert Ruger was married in prison, about four years earlier. The woman sitting in front of me had met Ruger on the Internet, through a Web site for people on death row searching for pen pals. He had posted his picture and biographical information on the site and this woman responded to him. In that Web page photo, Ruger held an afghan that he had knitted. His handicraft, and his smile, had attracted this woman, and the two wrote letters back and forth, developing a relationship. Ruger offered her advice on raising her children and helped her, from prison, with some daily chores such as balancing her checkbook. The couple had been married for four years when I met her that day, and for all four of those years Ruger was waiting to die.

Ruger's wife turned her gaze from the wall to me and asked, "So—what kind of research are you doing down here?"

I told her that I was there for just what I was doing at that moment: talking to family members involved in executions. I added, "I'm also here to witness a man named Edward Castro be executed in a couple of hours." What I didn't tell them was that six days ago I sat in my office debating whether I should watch Castro die, or their father/husband/brother be killed. Until my encounter with his family in the restaurant, I hadn't thought of Ruger as a real person, only as a killer waiting to die. Meeting his relatives opened my eyes to an aspect of executions that I hadn't thought about; the effect they have on the family of the condemned.

The four children returned to the table and the only one that seemed to notice that a strange man was talking to her family was the teenage girl. She looked at me with the same look that teens give to just about every adult: a mixture of disgust and contempt. Ruger's daughter, the woman with the photo on her shirt, explained that the small children who had just returned from the display case of toys were Ruger's grandchildren. I nodded and smiled.

One of the little kids again asked Ruger's sister for money to buy toys from the glass case. The woman, with hardly a glance down at the child, said, "I already told you 'no,' now don't ask again." The child looked crushed and defeated, and went back to sit with the other kids and to plot out a new strategy for getting the money. The children were clearly frustrated that their continual appeals were met with almost no consideration.

In this respect, the children's unsuccessful attempts to gain the trinkets under the glass by the cash register mirrored their parent's efforts to save Ruger from death. Like their children, the adults talked among themselves about what they wanted and selected one person to go to the authorities and beg once again for Ruger's life. They would put on their best behavior and argue, with all of the rationality they could muster, why their request should be granted. Then the authorities would say something like, "No, I already told you what my decision is. Now, please, don't ask again." Like their children did, the parents would re-group, talk about how unfair and cruel the authorities were being and, even though they were already told "no," would again approach the authorities and appeal for what they wanted.

At best, the parents would hear from the authorities "We'll see, hold on a minute," and their hopes would be raised, thinking that they may get what they want this time. But instead they would be told, "We have decided to wait for a month and think about it again." To the parents, this was better than simply being told no. But it was only a temporary solution and the parents' appeal would probably again be denied.

As I thought about these two similar appeal processes, another child approached Ruger's wife and asked, "Then, can we have some money for gum instead?"

The woman answered, with little thought, "No, honey, just sit down and eat your ice cream."

I knew that children would always continue their requests because parents always seemed to have control over what they want. Likewise, the parents would continue their appeals to the State of Florida, because it had control over what *they* wanted. In all likelihood, neither group was very likely to get what they truly desired. To the decision-makers (the *parents* for the children and the *State* for the parents), granting the request simply isn't the best thing to do. And in neither case will the plaintiffs ever understand the decision or view it as "fair." But regardless, children will always ask and will always be let down when they are told "no," and family members will also always ask and will also be hurt and disappointed when they are told "no." Fairness and justice, it seems, are subjective matters.

I asked the family where they lived. Ruger's sister lived on the East Coast, several states to the north. His wife lived in the upper Midwest and I remembered that I already knew that from reading a newspaper article about their marriage. I thought about how far they lived from the prison and Robert Ruger. "It must get very expensive driving down to Florida all the time," I remarked.

"We do what we have to do," Ruger's sister replied strongly. "If it was *your* family in there, *you* would do whatever you could, too."

Another thought occurred to me, but I didn't share this one. I imagined that it must be incredibly frightening and stressful to pack up the car with the kids and drive for several days to see if Grandpa is going to be killed or not. Upon finding out that he is going to live a while longer, they spend a few days visiting him and then drive home. Then they come back and do the whole thing again in another month. Of course they could skip a month, but that might be the month that the State actually kills the man.

I also thought about the financial costs of this ordeal for the condemned killer's family. They would have to take time off from work, assuming they still have a job to go back to each time. They would incur the costs of gas, motels, food, and other travel expenses. I was beginning to understand, at least in a small part, their frustration. But without having a close family member waiting to die on death row, I could never fully comprehend the longing and the pain.

"So what do you do with your research? Write, like, books and things?" Ruger's daughter asked me.

"Well, I haven't written a book yet," I explained. "I usually write research articles that are published in academic journals which most people never read. But I am thinking about writing a book about this whole experience."

"You should. You need to tell the world about what they do to them in there," Ruger's wife interjected, with both conviction and anger. "Tell how his family is tortured and how we die everyday he sits in there waiting on death row."

To be honest, I had not thought much about the family of the inmate. I had intended to try to talk to the family members of *victims*, not those of their killer. I hadn't even considered the amount of pain and suffering that the kin of condemned prisoners must go through every day.

We spent a little more time talking together, and then I thanked them for their time and wished them "good luck," though I don't know what I meant by that. It just seemed like the thing to say. I returned to my table and my now room-temperature food. Robert Ruger's family picked up their personal items, checked the table to see if they had forgotten anything, and left without saying goodbye to me. I watched them go up to the counter, pay for their food, and walk out the door.

I would never see Ruger's family again.

One month later, back in my office in Minnesota, I read that Robert D. Ruger had been executed by lethal injection at Florida State Prison in Starke.

CHAPTER SIXTEEN

By 3:25 p.m., I was back in my motel room, showered and dressed, hopefully like a professional execution witness. I sat on the motel bed staring at the cheap, digital clock on the night stand. I thought of Castro, as I had done endlessly, in one way or another, for the last six days. Did Castro have a clock in his prison cell? If so, was he sitting there by himself, staring as the remaining hours of his ruined life ticked away?

This was the day Castro had probably thought about, nonstop, for the last twelve years. Did he wake up every morning and, in those first few moments of sleepy confusion, think to himself, "Is this my time? Is it happening today?" Did he then remember that no, it wasn't time yet? Each day he came closer to his death, but today wasn't the day. Would he get out of bed, use the toilet, brush his teeth, shave, eat, and maybe change his clothes? Or did he wonder, "Why bother?" Why go through the motions of living just to wait for death?

If each of us were forced to think about our own impending death, we would have a life similar to that of a person on death row. We would be defined by our impending death and would see life as nothing more than a "predeath" state. Life would be nothing more than a series of actions that we take to fill our days while waiting for our death. Every day we would stare at the wall knowing that the end creeps closer with each tick of the second hand on a prison official's clock.

Tick ... Tick ... Tick ...

We are closer to death than we were just a few seconds before.

Tick ... Tick ... Tick ...

In that length of time, hundreds of people all over the world have just died

Tick ... Tick ... Tick ...

Somewhere, an old man dies peacefully in his sleep, dreaming of adventures long past.

Tick ... Tick ... Tick ...

A middle-aged woman dies in a hospital bed, surrounded by brave-faced family members.

Tick ... Tick ... Tick ...

A tiny baby in her mother's womb is trying to be born. She feels a firm pull around her neck and gently drifts away forever with the umbilical cord still wrapped around her throat.

Tick ... Tick ... Tick ...

A poor farmer in Nigeria lies down on the floor of his grass hut and sweats and grunts as a virus ravages his body. In a final glorious second, he relaxes and closes his eyes.

Tick ... Tick ... Tick ...

A teenage boy in Ireland is driving his mum's car for only the fourth time. He panics when the wheels of the car hit a sheet of water on the road. He jerks the wheel and sends the car head-on into a delivery truck, killing him before he has time to scream.

Tick ... Tick ... Tick ...

Edward Castro in Starke, Florida stares at the brick wall of his cell.

Tick ... Tick ... Tick ...

He is dying.

Tick ... Tick ... Tick ...

I kneel in my hotel room praying for strength and praying for protection for my family and myself. I thank the Lord that I have traveled thousands of miles today without being harmed, and I ask Him to continue to watch over me until I get home. When I get home, I will pray that He will protect my family and me throughout the night and the following day. I do this at least once a day, everyday.

I know that someday He will have to ignore my request.

Tick ... Tick ... Tick ...

As I left my motel room that afternoon, I noted to myself that when I returned later, Castro would be dead. Castro would be dead and I will have watched it happen. I climbed into the rental car and pointed it south on the highway. I looked for the large sign that said, "Florida State Prison," as two different people had told me that I "can't miss it." Sure enough, I saw it right where they said it would be, and I turned onto a two-lane road.

The tree-lined avenue was flanked by homes on either side and I immediately noticed a large number of churches along the route, as well. The stretch of road to the prison was less than ten miles long, but it passed dozens of churches. All the different denominations of Christianity must have been represented; some of which I had never heard of before. A few of the churches were magnificent buildings, set far back from the road. They had large parking lots beside them to accommodate the flocks and flocks of faithful who gathered there. Other churches I passed were only large enough to hold ten or 20 people at the very most.

I saw a motel that had been turned into a church, a gas station that had been turned into a church, and what looked like a large phone booth or ATM vestibule that had been turned into a church. I wondered, "Why all the churches?" With the prison and its regular executions nearby, perhaps the churches were there to provide comfort, like mothers in public places who sometimes flock around the crying babies of strangers.

I thought about the institution of religion and how some adherents to Christianity in the South support the death penalty while maintaining their strong Christian views. I found this concept both interesting and confusing, because it seems to be a contradiction to me. Jesus had been pretty clear about the ideas of turning the other cheek and his commandment not to meet violence with more violence. I didn't think he meant that we should allow killers to wander the streets, victimizing our loved ones. But I was certain that he didn't intend for his followers to kill all the sinners. On the cross, Jesus asked God to forgive his killers. He didn't say, "Father, kill them all for they are murdering me."

I am not a biblical scholar, but I don't think that one can use the nonviolent teachings of Jesus Christ as support for the death penalty and expect to have any credibility. It wasn't clear to me whether Christians in the South believed that Christianity promoted, or simply tolerated, executions. Did they believe the death penalty was necessary to ensure a more Christ-like community for the law-abiding citizens?

As I drove further from town and toward the prison, the asphalt road widened and became a highway. On the right side of the road, a large, red sign announced I was entering an area with prisons and prisoners. It advised me to be careful, which seemed like good advice.

Just past the sign, the trees lining both sides of the road disappeared, leaving an expanse of grassy fields nearly a mile long and at least a half mile wide. It looked as though the trees simply quit growing and left nearly one square mile of brown grass, with a highway going through the middle. Sitting on both sides of the road were several prisons. The facilities looked remarkably different from one another, but they all managed to project the cold feeling that seems to emanate from every state penitentiary.

About a quarter of a mile beyond the last tree, a small complex of buildings sat on the right side of the road. The sign out front identified the grayish-white structures as a "Youth Facility." It looked like a typical camp with dorm-room style housing. Surrounding the buildings was a fence that didn't look all that difficult to climb, if one were desperate enough.

On the left side of the road, and set back several hundred yards, was a series of massive, green buildings, each three or four stories tall. Even from the distance, the fence surrounding the buildings looked impenetrable. I noticed a small, red brick building set slightly away from the rest of the green ones. As I drove further down the highway that ran parallel to the prison, I could see that this red structure actually sat outside the fence that surrounded the rest of the complex. I drove slowly, trying to get a better look. With all the buildings in the immediate area, I couldn't tell if this was my prison or not. But it looked larger, and more heavily guarded, than any of the other complexes in the area.

I noticed a short road that led from this complex to the highway and masses of police and civilian cars had gathered at the point where the two roads met. Cars were parked on both sides of the highway and still others lined up in front of a closed gate. Uniformed police officers walked about on the highway and among the parked cars. I suspected that this prison, which was the center of commotion, was my final destination. I slowed my car down and turned left onto the short road, heading toward a guardhouse. A large sign arched over the road and told me I had arrived at the "Florida State Prison."

I pulled in behind another car and was third in line to get into the prison. I didn't know how many people usually waited at the gate, but the staggering number of police and prison guards in the area suggested that something unusual was taking place. It was hard to tell how many there were for sure, but I counted approximately 20 to 30 police officers and prison guards in the vicinity. They wore several different types of uniforms and walked about near the gate area or stood around the cars that waited in line. As each car pulled forward toward the gate, 3 or 4 police officers would approach the car and talk with the driver. Several times I saw identification change hands and one of the officers would search a piece of paper on the clipboard he held before the car was permitted to pass. I moved one more car forward and sat waiting, staring at the "Florida State Prison" sign.

Here it was. This is where people came to die. I had thought about this place every waking moment for nearly a week. I had even dreamt about it. And there it sat waiting to admit me.

I scanned the scene before me: the sun starting its decent toward dusk, the prison sign arching over the road, the cars waiting in front of me, the uniformed officers milling around. From my backpack on the seat beside me, I pulled out my camera, a 35mm auto-focus with a zoom lens. As I sat inside the rental car, I snapped a photo of my view from behind the steering wheel.

Almost instantly, several police officers descended on my car, all yelling at me. I panicked and only caught bits and pieces of the commands they shouted my direction.

"STOP TAKING PICTURES, NOW!"
"WHAT ARE YOU DOING HERE?"
"WHO ARE YOU?"
"GIVE ME THAT CAMERA!"

The officer with the clipboard was still ahead, motioning for the car in front of me to proceed. Suddenly, he began waving excitedly, ordering me to approach the gate at once. As I did, the other officers yelled to him, though he was only five feet away, that I had been taking pictures. His response was more fitting for someone who approached the gate with a bomb or a machine gun, instead of a cheap, discount-store camera.

With several officers standing around him for reinforcement, the cop with the clipboard hollered into my face, "What are you doing here? Why are you taking pictures? Who are you?" He didn't give me any time to answer the first question before asking the second, and then the third.

I wanted them to stop screaming at me, so I tried to respond in a way that made me appear important. "I am Dr. Joseph Diaz," I announced, trying to hide my fear and embarrassment. "I have been asked by the State of Florida to serve as a witness at the execution of Edward Castro."

"Give me some I.D!" the cop demanded, without even the slightest bit of respect. I handed him my driver's license and watched as he read every line on it. Then he commanded, "Give me some other form of I.D!" This time I offered my faculty identification card from the university, as well as a business card. He wrote down the information from all three items but still was not satisfied. He must have thought I was not Dr. Diaz. Or perhaps he believed that I was Dr. Diaz, but Dr. Diaz was not supposed to be there.

He shifted gears slightly but maintained his hostile tone of voice, "Why were you taking pictures?"

I still wanted him to stop yelling at me. I tried to sound as innocent as possible in my reply, "Because I am a professor of criminology and I study this sort of thing." I knew I hadn't really answered his question, but I was nervous and seeking some common ground with the man. I hoped he would see me as one of the good guys and stop treating me as if I were a prisoner who had somehow escaped and was now trying to get back into prison. I quickly added, "I wanted to take a photo of the sign above the gate. There is a photo of it on the Florida State Prison Web site, but I just wanted to take my own." I didn't mention that I also wanted to get all of the police officers standing around the cars as they waited to go into the prison.

One of the back-up officers piped in, "Yeah, that's true. I've seen that photo."

The cop with the clipboard softened slightly, "What else did you photograph?"

I wanted to tell him, "Secret Pentagon files. You had better arrest me." Thinking he might actually do it, I told him the truth. "That's it, just the sign. Am I not supposed to take pictures or something?"

He rolled his eyes and looked at me as if I was far too stupid to be breathing by myself, "No you can't take pictures," he snapped. "There's an execution today!"

Now it was my turn to make him feel foolish and I calmly told him, "I know there's an execution today. That's why I'm here. I am serving as an Official Witness for the State."

He turned around and walked into a small guard shack and came back out with a different sheet of paper. He read it closely and appeared to find what he was looking for. Next he compared my driver's license and my faculty ID card to something on his paper. Then looked at me and asked, "Are you Dr. Joseph Diaz?"

I was certain that he hadn't really forgotten my name. I suspected that he was just trying to do his job as thoroughly as possible. This both impressed and irritated me at the same time. This is the type of cop you want on the streets protecting you, but not the one you want to pull you over if you have been speeding ... or taking pictures of a state prison on an execution day. "Yes, I'm Dr. Diaz," I answered.

He continued, "And you are from Minnesota?"

I thought about telling him, "No, I am actually from Illinois, but my father and ancestors are from Mexico. I was raised in Illinois and Arizona, and went to school in Arizona, Utah and Las Vegas. I've really only lived in Minnesota for about a year and a half; so no, I'm not from Minnesota." I didn't say this because I was afraid that if I did, he would want to see some proof that I had actually lived in all of those places. Instead, I simply answered, "Yeah, I'm from Minnesota." And then I added, for at least the third time so far, "I am here to serve as a witness at the Castro execution." I threw that last part in to remind him that I had been invited to come here, and that I would like to get on with it. I truly thought that he was not going to let me in.

But the cop with the clipboard gave me back my ID, not even keeping my business card. Next, he instructed me to follow the road to the red, brick building I had seen earlier. There I was to check in at the warden's office. And finally, before he motioned for me to drive on, he leaned a little closer to the car and stated, much to my surprise, "You can keep the photo you took, but don't take any more today or we'll confiscate your camera. I should take it right now, but if you're a professor, I'll let you hold on to it." He truly did say that last part.

CHAPTER SEVENTEEN

As I pulled away from the guard shack and headed toward the warden's office, I saw the highway on my left side and the prison fence on my right. Now a little closer to it, I could see the fence's imposing height. It looked about 18 feet high and appeared to have razor blade-imbedded barbed wire across its top. An exact duplicate stood about 15 to 20 feet inside the first fence. If a prisoner climbed over one of the fences to escape, he had only a few seconds to enjoy his accomplishment before he had to do it all over again.

I found a parking space in a lot the size of a football field. Four o'clock must have been "the changing of the guards" at the prison. All around me employees left their cars and walked toward the fence, where a guard stood at a gate approximately 50 feet from the front door to the warden's office. I followed the crowd and found myself walking alongside a middle-aged prison guard. I said hello to the rather heavy-set man.

"Hey there," he replied, beaming a broad smile. "You here for the execution?"

"Yes, I am," I confirmed.

"Are you a reporter?" he wanted to know. I must have looked like a reporter, because I had heard that same question in Denny's just a couple of hours before.

"No, I'm a professor," I told him. "I'm pretty sure reporters make more money than me." He laughed and nodded in agreement, as though he had seriously considered becoming a professor, but decided against it when he learned how little we were paid. We parted without saying goodbye. The guard walked toward the gate as I entered the red, brick building.

On the other side of the door, I walked into a sparsely furnished reception area, with a counter and one woman sitting behind it. "Florida State Prison," she said to me as I approached the counter. I thought this was an odd way to greet someone in person, and then I quickly realized that she was answering the phone. The receptionist wore one of those telephone head-sets that slips over the user's ear and has a mouthpiece extending in front. This allows one to talk on the phone and look cool at the same time. I pretended that I had known this all along.

The woman then looked at me directly and asked, "Can I help you?" She didn't smile, but that was OK, since the guard I had just met in the parking lot had given me a smile big enough to carry me through the rest of the day.

"Yes, I am Dr. Joseph Diaz and I am here to watch the Castro execution," I told her. I was getting tired of repeating that line, but people kept asking. Then I ventured, "Things seem a little ... uh ... tense around here today."

She smiled slightly, reassuring me, "It's always like that when we have executions." She referred to a sheet of paper, found my name, and sent me down a short hallway toward the warden's office.

It was 3:50 p.m. when I came to the only open doorway in the hall and passed through it. An over-sized desk dominated the office that I entered. Among the clutter, I saw a nameplate that read, "Sarah Harper," and realized that this was the woman I had spoken with by telephone six days earlier.

Ms. Harper was pretty and I guessed her age to be in the early 40s. She flashed a warm and genuine smile and I instantly liked her. I looked around her small office, noting lots of plants, several knickknacks, a few popular hardcover books, and stacks and stacks of files, that nearly covered all the empty spaces on the floor. Also in the tiny office, standing with his arm on a particleboard bookcase, was a well-groomed man who appeared to be about 40, but was most likely ten years older than that. His hair was perfect and he looked more like United States Senator Trent Lott than Senator Trent Lott himself. I had met people before who could pass for a celebrity in a dark room when everyone was drunk. But this guy could very easily have been Senator Lott. While I suspected that the man wasn't the Senator, I still kept finding myself wondering.

I introduced myself and stood in the small space that remained in the tiny office after the large desk and "Senator Lott" had claimed their spots. Ms. Harper smiled and offered me her hand. It was the kindest reception I had received since leaving the Ruger family at Denny's and arriving at the prison. "It is sure nice to meet you, Dr. Diaz," she said warmly. "Thank you very much for agreeing to serve."

I didn't know how to respond. The standard line, "It is my pleasure" didn't seem like the right thing to say, nor was it the truth. So instead I replied, "Thank you for having me." I should have been a politician.

Ms. Harper introduced me to "Senator Lott," who turned out to be David Anders, a Florida State Highway Patrol Officer. I found it easy to talk with this man, and soon learned that Anders had witnessed one other execution, that one by electrocution, three years before. Because he seemed so relaxed and confident in that environment, I quickly tried to develop a bond with him.

In my sociology work at the university, I study human interactions and the relationships people form. Human beings have the need to feel connected to one another. Researchers believe that during stressful periods or in frightening situations, individuals who might otherwise never say a word to each other often become close friends.

Times of stress make us feel vulnerable and we respond by doing things to make ourselves feel more secure. Those actions can vary widely, from physically touching strangers to sharing intimate details about ourselves to quickly establishing trust with others.

Eventually, I would learn that David was 25 years older than I was and that our life experiences were not at all similar. But during those few hours at the prison that afternoon, he was my best friend. I did not leave his side until later that evening when it was all over and we got in our cars and parted company. I felt emotionally closer to him than I had ever felt toward another man, at any other time in my life.

David and I sat talking with Ms. Harper for about 20 minutes. Apparently the two of us were the first two witnesses to arrive and we both felt a little bit out of place. As we waited for the others, Ms. Harper kept the conversation going. She first asked me, "So, what type of research do you do?"

I gave my usual canned response for such situations, telling her that I worked in the areas of crime and social problems, but that I had also done work on the issue of suicide. David politely listened.

"So, are you going to write a book about this?" she wanted to know next. I noticed that she began most of her questions with the word "so." This might have been a personal habit, but I got the idea that she wasn't sure who I was and exactly why I was there, which made two of us.

"I don't know if I will write a book about this or not," I answered truthfully. This was the second time that day I had been asked that question, earlier by the Ruger family and now by this prison administrator. "It wouldn't surprise me, but I am not planning on it."

Ms. Harper continued to ask me questions. She wanted to know about my education, my life in Minnesota, and other such personal details. Clearly she was a person who took a genuine interest in other people, and was not simply trying to fill the silence in the tiny office. This was a welcome change from the mostly harsh reception I'd received so far at this institution.

As I told Ms. Harper my life story and David stood listening, suddenly a door on the other side of the room opened. A short, stocky and very bald man quickly emerged from the warden's office and walked right past me. He disappeared into the hallway without uttering a single word to any of us. Ms. Harper neither commented, nor appeared to even notice.

Moments later, the same man re-entered the small space, this time with two other men in tow. All three of them passed within two feet of me, yet none of them acknowledged my presence. They walked into the warden's office and closed the door behind them. Two hours later I would see these men again, inside the death chamber.

In between answering questions about me, I asked Ms. Harper a few of my own. I learned that she, too, had served as a witness to an execution, several years before. She explained to me that at the time, she had been working in the prison for a couple of years and she felt that she should probably see for herself exactly what happens on the other side of the door to the death house. The condemned murderer had been electrocuted and this sweet and motherly administrative assistant had watched him die. I respected her willingness to go through that.

Soon an older man, dressed in a black leather suit coat, walked in and announced that he, too, was there for the execution. By that time, Ms. Harper's small office was already at capacity, so the new arrival was directed to a conference room just across the hallway. David and I were invited to join him and we all walked the short distance together.

At that point, the strangest day of my life suddenly became even stranger. I hadn't really thought about what I expected to see in a room where people wait to witness an execution. But I was stunned to walk into a room full of tables covered with food. There were party platters of sandwiches, cookies, fruits and vegetables, coolers of drinks, and condiments. The place looked like it might be the scene of a large Fourth of July picnic.

The food and drinks created a relaxed atmosphere and the gathering quickly began to feel like a small social event. Every new "guest" that arrived was greeted with a hearty, "Come on in!" People mingled and talked. One witness was a bit of a jokester and he kept everyone entertained. Waiters in uniforms, prison guard uniforms, catered to the group, encouraging everyone to relax and enjoy all the food.

I began to get upset with the casual indifference the other witnesses were displaying. This was not supposed to be a party and I refused to relax and act like it was. I could not stop thinking that in some other part of that very prison, a man was staring at a clock and counting down the last two hours of his life, wondering what was going to happen to him when he entered the death chamber. Meanwhile, the sentinels of death were eating, drinking, and generally being merry, obviously denying to themselves and others the actual reason we were all there. Conversations ebbed and flowed, the food slowly disappeared, and friendships were made. It was surreal.

As the remaining witness arrived and joined the party, I scanned the room. I was clearly the youngest one there, and as far as I could tell, I was the only person *not* somehow involved in law enforcement. Several of the witnesses were retired police officers, including one man named Bill. Bill, a retired narcotics officer, had long gray hair that he pulled back into a ponytail that hung well below his shoulders. I had never before seen an older man with a ponytail, and the effect was one more of desperation for lost youth than a statement of fashion. He was sitting in a chair across from me, on the other side of a wide conference table.

We had not met or talked since he came into the room, but completely out of the blue he asked me, "So, Doctor, why do people kill each other?"

The room got very quiet, as most of the conversations stopped. Nearly all of the 15 or so witnesses and guards looked in our direction. Bill, I had heard him tell someone earlier, had been a police officer and I suspected he had already come to his own conclusion about the causes of murder. Still, I felt that his question was genuine and that he sincerely wanted *my* opinion on the matter.

"I believe most murders are the result of greed and pride," I told him. "They are, like everything else in complex human behavior, learned in some form or another. For the murderer, killing another individual either satisfies his economic needs or his sexual fantasies, or it serves to avenge a perceived wrong. Ultimately, these motives are all a form of pride or greed. The killer feels his own desires are more important than the life of his or her victim."

Bill silently considered my response for a moment, as he played with the toothpick in his mouth. Those who had directed their attention to us moments before now returned to their own conversations. He leaned forward, over his plate of finger food, and said, "That's an interesting theory, but I think killers are simply evil and mean people. They're like animals, with no sense of guilt or remorse."

"I think they are humans, just like you and I," I disagreed, "but they either ignore their guilt, or, because of past events in their lives, they have never learned to care enough about someone else that the emotion of guilt even exists for them."

Before Bill could comment on my last argument, a uniformed guard came in the conference room and announced it was time to go. The conversations instantly stopped and the somber mood quickly returned. I looked at my watch: It was 5:15 p.m. I maneuvered through the group to reach the side of my friend, David.

"OK … here we go," I nervously whispered to him.

He softly smiled at me but didn't say a word, as the twelve of us witnesses walked down the hall and out the front door of the red brick warden's office into the late afternoon sun.

CHAPTER EIGHTEEN

The guard led our group across a one-lane asphalt road where we approached the enormous razor-blade-embedded barricades. The fences were intimidating when I first saw them upon my arrival at the prison, but when one stepped *into* the area between the fences, their frightening effect was much more pronounced. They were 18 to 20 feet tall and, literally, covered over, every inch, with double-edged, barbed razor blades. There were also 5 feet high coils of razor-sharp barbed wire at the base of the fence, which would not permit an inmate to even get close enough to *attempt* to climb the fence without bleeding to death.

The whole horrible monstrosity was present again just 15 to 20 feet away. In the rare event that an inmate scaled the inside fence and lived to get down the other side, which seemed impossible for me to imagine, he would have to do it again seconds later as he approached the outside fence. This being done, of course, with the guards in the tower shooting 30-caliber bullets at them as they tried to climb over. It looked like it would be easier for an inmate to escape by building a full-size helicopter out of plastic forks and toilet paper rolls and then flying out, rather than trying to climb the fence.

After passing through both of the two frightening fences, we entered the front door of another building. With its pale green color and masonry block construction, the prison looked like it had been constructed around the time of World War II. Inside, we again showed our identification and approached a metal detector. The first six witnesses passed through the screening device without a problem. Then it was my turn.

I was nervous, even though I had only once before set off a metal detector, and that occurred years earlier after I had left my keys in my pocket as I walked through airport security. It was embarrassing and I found that ever since that one adverse incident, my heart always beats a little faster whenever I have to go through one of those things.

I put my keys and watch in the bowl next to the machine and stepped through. Alarms rang loudly, further reinforcing my metal-detector anxiety. Evidently metal detectors can be adjusted to different levels of sensitivity, and this one was obviously set as high as possible.

I was asked to take off my suit coat and belt, which I did, and walk through the detector another time. Again it went off. Next, a guard with a hand-held unit scanned my entire body, including those parts that I didn't particularly want radioactive instruments near. Still, they could not find the source of metal. One of the guards suggested that it might be my dental fillings. I was *not* going to re-move those, regardless of their security protocols.

The other witnesses, including David, began to look annoyed with me. I felt like I was letting them down in some way. I began to worry that I might have to completely undress in front of them all before they would let me through. Finally guards instructed me to take off my shoes, and my tie, and to step through the detector once gain. As I was removing my shoes, David passed through the de-tector without incident.

Luckily, the culprit was finally determined to be the little metal eyelets in my shoes, and *not* a weapon that I was trying to smuggle in. The metal detector was *that* sensitive. I was anxious to get my clothes back on and join the group on the other side of the detector. One of the two remaining witnesses also had problems gaining clear-ance and I, along with the others in the group, acted an-noyed that he was holding us up.

Adequately screened and surrounded by guards, we walked the short 30 feet or so down the hallway to the employee lunchroom. Along the way we passed a room surrounded by thick safety glass. Inside were video monitors, computers and several uniformed guards. The guards all stared at us but then quickly looked away when some of our group met their gaze. En route to the lunchroom, our escorts unlocked two more sets of prison bars, running from floor to ceiling, and allowed us to pass through.

In a space that looked like it could hold 200 to 300 people, our small group found more snacks and drinks waiting for us. To unknowing outsiders, the scene might have looked like a high school dance We were all wearing our best clothes, feeling tense and awkward and standing around in a large, institutional-looking lunchroom, complete with punch and cookies, chaperones, and nervous guys who were uncomfortable wearing neckties.

Once again it appeared to be time to mingle. I had already talked to each of the other witnesses at least once and had learned that none of them were family members of Edward Castro. Prison officials must keep family members separate from the official witnesses, or perhaps none of Castro's family was even present for the end of his life. I had assumed that I would see people crying and begging the warden to let Castro live. Then it occurred to me that I had not seen family members of the killer's victims either. I had imagined the victim's families crying, too, but they would be encouraging the warden to hurry up the execution. But little this day was going as I had thought it would.

At a round, lunchroom table, David and I discussed the current state of the criminal justice system in America. Our conversation drifted from prison overcrowding, to plea bargains, and eventually to the death penalty, which was the subject I had been gently trying to direct our dialogue toward since we had first met two hours earlier. Judging by the words and phrases I had heard him use back at the picnic in the conference room, I already knew that he personally viewed the death penalty as justice for the victims, who could no longer defend themselves. Finally, I asked him directly, "Are you in favor of the death penalty?"

In a firm tone of voice he replied, "Given my Christian beliefs, I think we need the death penalty."

"Are you a strong Christian?" I asked him.

Without thinking about it, and quickly nodding his head, he answered, "Yes, sir, I am."

"I'm a Christian, too," I shared with him. "But I can't see how that should be a basis for executing people. To me, it seems that executions were not even addressed by Christ, and more than likely, they offended him."

David was noticeably disturbed by my comment. He looked up at me and defensively argued, "There are some guys in here, right here in this same prison that I locked up." He told me passionately, "Some guys that, if I told you what they did, you would *want* them to be executed. You wouldn't be able to sleep at night if these people were on the streets."

"It sounds like you are talking about someone in particular," I coaxed. "Do you know someone on death row in this prison?"

David answered my question by telling me a disturbing story about what happened when he was a rookie Florida State Highway Patrol Officer. He recounted the story, which still haunts me to this day, as he stared at a wall in the lunchroom. One afternoon, he spotted a van with a broken taillight as he was driving down a highway on his patrol. As was the routine, he signaled for the van to pull over to the side of the road, and approached the side of the van where the driver had rolled down his window to speak with him.

As David stepped up to the open window he immediately smelled blood. The stench of human remains was so strong and distinct that he instantly recognized it. He knew something bad had happened in that van. The young state trooper drew his service weapon and ordered the driver out of the vehicle. He didn't know exactly what was inside, but he did know that it wasn't going to be good.

He escorted the driver back to the patrol car, and that's when he noticed blood dripping onto the ground from the back doors of the van. Whatever was inside had lost so much blood that it was actually pouring out of the cracks in the doors, onto the pavement. When David had the driver cuffed and under control, he took a deep breath, and looked inside the van. He told me what he found inside was the single worst thing he had ever seen in his life.

When David opened the doors, he found the butchered body of a preteen girl. The driver had ripped out her internal organs and cut off her arms, legs, and head. She was lying in pieces, in the back of the van where he had slaughtered her.

It was later learned that this young girl was the man's step-daughter and that he had abducted and raped her before eviscerating her with a knife. The man was on his way to dump the body and clean up the van when David, simply by chance, pulled him over for a broken taillight. The driver of the van was sentenced to die in the Florida State Prison, the very same one David and I were sitting in two decades later, debating the death penalty.

He was visibly shaken from reliving the experience as he shared his story with me. "Were you at the trial?" I asked him.

"Yes, sir, I was," he answered, still livid with anger at the driver of the van. "I was there every day and I testified against him. I almost cheered when he was sentenced to die."

"So you *want* this guy to die?" I asked, even though I already knew the answer.

"I want to be right there when they kill him," he told me, in a very matter-of-fact tone of voice. "I want to look into his face, when he knows he is dying, and watch him suffer. I want to see him scared and knowing he is about to go burning into Hell. If they asked me to, I would throw the switch to kill him."

But then I detected a change in his tone of voice. I heard contempt when he said, "If he dies now, they'll give him a lethal injection, but I want him to fry. If they asked me to, I would hold a gun to his head and blow his brains out."

I was jarred by the discovery of this man's quiet rage. Earlier, I had found David to be pleasant and kind. Cautiously, I asked with a hint of doubt in my voice, "You would actually *kill* him if they asked you to?"

"Absolutely," he stated with total conviction. "I would kill him in a minute. After what he did to that poor little girl? After what I saw? Yes sir, I would sure do it."

Our conversation cooled a bit after that exchange. David was perceptive and he could tell that I didn't share his anger or his need for violent revenge. I was tempted to judge this man as another extremist who refused to look at the world objectively. I wanted to feel morally superior to him, but I couldn't.

The fact was, David had seen things in his life that I had only *read* about. I knew that I could not handle his job, seeing what he saw every day, and still hope to remain sane. He was the type of person I would call if I were scared or felt threatened. I would know that he would pro-tect me.

Unlike me, who taught middle-class kids in orderly classrooms, David worked amid the violent filth of soci-ety, watching its destruction for decades. He faced deci-sions that I would never have to make. He has had to ask himself, "Do I ever want to arrest this monster again? Can I protect the people I'm paid to safeguard with this *thing* on the street?"

The answer David heard in his head was, "no." So he decided to do whatever it took to ensure that criminals he apprehended were never able to harm others again. I had a tremendous amount of respect for his desire to protect civilians, people like me, in the best way he knew how.

From across the table, I watched David eat a cookie and stare into his glass of fruit punch. He was as close to a hero as I had ever known. This man was driven by the fear that something unthinkable would happen to an innocent person, and that he should have prevented it. While I disagreed with David politically and morally, I clearly understood his position and respected him for it.

The festive atmosphere present in the warden's office was replaced by a quiet, anxious mood shared by everyone. Like me, the other witnesses began checking their watches more and more frequently as time wore on. Although it had barely been discussed, we all knew why we were there. Even to the witnesses who had already seen this process before, the occasion was still regarded as both significant and ominous. We were going to watch a man die and none of us were pretending any more that we were there for any other reason.

One hundred yards away, in another part of the complex, Edward Castro sat in his prison cell. The brutal serial killer talked quietly with his spiritual advisor; a man named Dan. Earlier that day, Castro had visited with his family for the last time and said his goodbyes to everyone who loved him and kept him in their prayers throughout his 12 years on death row. He had eaten his final meal and was now waiting for the moment that he had been thinking about every day for the last decade. He knew that in a matter of minutes, they were going to come for him and say, "OK, Edward, it's time."

He would then say goodbye to his spiritual advisor, Dan, who, with the witnesses, would watch Castro's execution. As anyone in his situation would be, Castro must have been incredibly nervous in a way that most of us will never understand. To make the execution easier for everyone involved, including the prison staff, he was given an injection of Valium to calm him. When the drug took effect, the killer became physically relaxed, but in no way was his ability to understand what was happening to him diminished. He knew what was waiting, and he sat and counted out the last few seconds of his ruined life.

Back in the part of the prison where I waited, a white paper napkin with store-bought cookies and a Dixie-cup full of tap water sat in front of me. I felt desperately lonely and out of place among these men for whom death and murder were common experiences. I wondered how I had gotten so far from home.

A uniformed guard then entered the lunchroom and announced, "We'll be going now. Please leave your food and drinks here and take your personal items with you."

All of us silently rose from our chairs and followed the man in a single file. As we made our way down the hall, prison guards, who were stationed every 20 feet or so, watched our procession with a degree of reverence. No one spoke to us, but it appeared that they all knew who we were and why we were there. We were doing a job that normal people didn't want to do, and we were doing it willingly. We had asked to serve in this position. We talked our way into this situation. We were the "Bringers of Death."

We reached the end of the wide concrete hallway where a prison guard opened a sealed iron door for us, letting in the late afternoon sun. I was confused to see that we were being led outside again and toward the back of the prison. In front of us, a metal stairway led down to the ground level. I didn't remember climbing any stairs, but I must have, because we were now about 20 feet above the rocky ground.

Stationed on the other side of the doorway were five police officers and prison guards. A few of the police officers nodded at us. I interpreted this as their way of showing appreciation for our service; perhaps for doing a job they didn't want to do.

As soon as the door to the stairway opened, I heard an explosion of voices, screams, and animal-like growls. The wave of frightening noise drowned out every other sound and was so loud that it seemed to be coming from every direction at once. I imagined thousands of caged animals, certainly not human beings, trapped inside a burning barn. The hair stood up on the back of my neck as I prepared to be attacked and killed by whatever creatures were screaming out in anger.

I nervously walked down the metal stairs without saying anything. Three passenger vans and several more uniformed officers waited at the bottom. I turned to one of the guards and asked, "What is that horrible sound?"

"It's the inmates," he replied, without elaborating.

"Are they always like this?" I asked, incredulously.

He answered my question without looking at me, "No, not always."

He was not in the mood to talk to me, but my genuine wonder pushed me on. "Do they sound like this because of the execution?" I tried.

Still looking everywhere but at me, the guard offered, "I guess so. Now please get inside the van, sir."

I wanted more information but clearly I wasn't going to get it from this man. Inside the van I selected a seat near the front. I leaned toward the driver and asked the same question, "Do the inmates always sound like this during executions?"

He was as somber as his partner outside the van, and merely responded quietly "Yes, sir." I wondered if I had said something to offend these men. Then it occurred to me that perhaps, for some reason, they were under orders to not talk with the witnesses.

I gave up and sat back in my seat. I watched the other passengers climb aboard the van. David climbed in right after me but, much to my disappointment, he sat near the back of the van. I didn't know where the van was headed but I felt uncomfortable asking any of the other witnesses. They had all done this before and no one seemed in the mood for chitchat.

I remembered that I had not ridden in this type of passenger van since I was an undergraduate student in Arizona. I was part of a group of pre-med students going to visit the medical school at the University of Arizona. We were all excited to get a taste of what medical school would be like. During the four-hour drive, we talked about the human anatomy lab and what it would look like to see a dead person laying in pieces on a metal gurney. I didn't know what I would see, but I never imagined that I would have difficulty seeing death presented in such a clinical and factual manner.

When our tour of the medical school concluded in the much-anticipated anatomy lab, I found myself in a room where the dead outnumbered the living by a ratio of nearly 2-to-1. We saw torsos with no limbs, heads without any faces, bodies with no skin, and unattached feet and hands. I had never seen human death up close before, and I began to seriously question my desire to become a physician.

Ten years later, I was again sitting in a passenger van, waiting to see death. But this time I would see the death occur, not just the aftermath.

Once all three vans were loaded with the witnesses, police officers and prison guards, we drove away from the main building. We turned right, driving past most of the light green, elongated halls that made up the prison. I wondered if we were leaving this prison complex to go to another one where the execution actually took place, but, again, I was afraid to ask anybody.

When we reached the last building, we turned right again and drove to a small structure connected to, but offset from, the rest of the prison. Off to the side of this small and inconspicuous square building was a white hearse. Two men were leaning on the hood of the car, smoking cigarettes. I noticed that they appeared to be waiting for something. At first the scene didn't fully register in my mind, but then it hit me.

These men were waiting for Castro after we were done with him.

After Edward Castro's death, they would enter the death chamber and collect his body. At that exact moment, as I rode in the passenger van and the men smoked cigarettes, Castro was a living man. But in a short time, he would no longer be a "man," but instead a "body." The hearse wasn't there to pick up *Castro* at all. They were waiting to pick up his spent and useless body, after I have watched it drained of its life.

They were waiting for me to watch him die. They waited to pick up the body, take it off to the morgue or wherever it was to go, and then go home to their wives and kids. It was nearly 6:00 p.m., and they probably wanted to punch out and head away from death for the next 12-14 hours. They probably just wanted the execution to simply hurry up so they could get on with their day.

They would do their job; I would do mine; Edward Castro would do his; and none of us would ever meet or see each other again.

CHAPTER NINETEEN

It was quickly getting darker now, as my watch ticked on toward 6 p.m. The three vans stopped in front of the short building and everybody stepped out into the early evening air. I noticed that at some point the other two vans had picked up a few more passengers. The newcomers exited the vans, just like the rest of us. However, instead of looking at the guards for cues as to what to do next, like we were, I saw them watching all of us – the witnesses.

I learned later that these people were counselors. They had been brought to the prison to assist us, the witnesses, in the event we needed to talk to someone after watching the execution. They were there to encourage us to talk about the experience, rather than quietly going home, drinking a bottle of rum, and committing suicide from the guilt of walking away from an execution alive. Everybody stood in a loose group outside the building where the vans had unloaded their cargo. We stared at the guards, at each other, or at the ground, waiting for whatever was to come next. I checked my watch: It was 5:42.

Just then, the building's only door opened and a prison guard with a clipboard stepped outside. "We will call you in alphabetically," he announced. "Please show your identification to the guard and then you will then be asked to sign a form." He didn't tell us what the form we would be signing was, but continued, "You will then enter the room and fill in the rows of chairs from front to back."

He then began calling out the names. My friend, David, was one of the first names to be called. In turn, each man stepped forward, showed his ID, entered the building and was directed to a room off to the right.   I couldn't see much from where I waited outside. It appeared that after each person entered the thick metal door, they had to immediately turn to the right and go through another door. I was straining my head to see what was inside the building when I heard my name called, "Diaz, Joseph D."

My heart leapt and I nervously stepped forward. I showed the guard my ID for what seemed like the hundredth time that day and signed the form that was presented to me. I didn't know what the form said, but I was not given the opportunity to read it. It was placed in my hands, and I was told "Sign here." Thinking it was probably important, I scribbled my signature on it. For all I knew, the paper I endorsed might have read, "The undersigned agrees to stand in and be executed if Mr. Edward Castro cannot be found or refuses to participate." I should have read it, but I was scared and would have done whatever they asked of me.

I stepped past the guard, turned to my immediate right and entered the infamous death chamber at the Florida State Prison. I was having difficulty breathing, which was an unusual sensation for a healthy 29-year-old man. I was surprised to see how small the place was. The room, constructed entirely of concrete and masonry block, looked about 15 feet long by, perhaps, 12 feet wide and another 9 feet high.

After passing the guard, I had entered from the back left corner of the room. I saw the four rows of chairs that the guard with the clipboard had referred to. The chairs looked cheap, like the kind in my low-budget hotel room. Their cloth seats were covered with a coarse, blue fabric. Because the area was so small, they were arranged closely together and were pushed as close to the front of the room as possible.

The chairs faced forward, away from me and toward the window that ran virtually the entire length of the room's front wall. The window began at the ceiling and continued down the wall to approximately 2 - 1/2 feet above the floor. There it met a short concrete wall. On the other side of the glass, a brown curtain covered the window and kept me from seeing what was on the other side.

I noticed the hum from the hidden ceiling fans and thought it seemed unusually loud. I remembered something I had read somewhere in my research that extra ceiling fans were installed to ventilate the area as much as possible because some witnesses tend to find the smell of burning human flesh during electrocutions is revolting.

Due to the alphabetic ordering, I was directed to the middle chair of the front row. I walked stiffly toward the glass wall and took my seat next to a witness named Lewis. The chairs were pushed so close to the observation window that my knees pressed up against the glass. They were giving me the best seat in the house. I tried to relax my chest and not let the witnesses around me hear my heavy breathing. My stomach, neck, and jaw were painfully tense, just like my chest. While I didn't exactly feel nauseated, my stomach did feel strange, as if it were loose, hard and quivering, all at the same time.

Lewis, the man I was seated next to, was a retired police officer and I guessed him to be in his 70s. I had met him at the gathering in the lunchroom earlier that afternoon. Lewis had witnessed several executions before this one, and I had said to him earlier, "It must be pretty bad seeing an execution in an electric chair."

"No, it's not bad," he told me. "Hell, if it wasn't for their hands clenching and twitching, you wouldn't even be able to tell they were being electrocuted."

"So the electrocutions you saw weren't bloody? The guy's face didn't catch on fire, or anything like that?" I asked him.

In a voice that revealed a little anger, he had answered, "No, it don't hurt them none at all! They're dead and they don't even feel nothing. Which is a lot better than they deserve and a lot better than their victims got."

As I approached Lewis in the death chamber, he looked up at me and gave me a kind smile, reassuring me that I was going to be all right and I didn't move my leg when it rested up against his in the tight space when I sat down. Normally I would feel awkward with my leg touching a strange man's leg, but I was willing to take whatever comfort being near him could offer. He didn't look like my kind old grandfather, but he was someone's grandfather and that helped. Lewis didn't move his leg either, but instead merely stared at the floor. After a couple of minutes he started quietly talking to David, who sat on the other side of him.

In the reflection in the glass before me, I watched the other witnesses entering the room behind me. The guard helped them find their seats and I noticed that he kept one chair of the front row unoccupied. After several minutes, four newspaper reporters entered along with a nonuniformed prison employee. They were instructed to take a seat in the back row, although other chairs closer, in the third row, were unoccupied. I concluded that the empty third row was probably reserved for family members, none of whom had come for Castro's final moments.

A few days after leaving Florida, I discovered a newspaper report on Castro's execution. It contained information about the execution that was not exactly true and I couldn't imagine why the reporter would write things that simply didn't happen. But I remembered that reporters sat in the back seats, behind two rows of people, where they probably couldn't see Castro or the execution very clearly at all. The reporter must have decided to improvise. Conversely, we were right up front and nothing stood between those of us in the front row and the man about to die.

After I watched the last reporter come in and be seated, the door through which we had all entered was closed and locked. We were locked inside the death chamber and we would not get out until we had watched a man being killed. Ted Bundy, the serial killer nicknamed "The Deliberate Stranger," Allen "Tiny" Davis, the 350-pound man who bled profusely during his electrocution, and Pedro Medina, the man who caught on fire during his execution, were all killed in the Florida State Prison. At that moment, I sat locked in a room that had seen more death and more murderers than I could begin to comprehend.

I wondered where Castro's family was? Why didn't they come? Maybe they had said their goodbyes earlier. Or perhaps they wanted to remember him as a living person rather than as a corpse laid out on a gurney. Or maybe they didn't care.

And what about the families of Castro's victims? Where were they? Did they feel that watching this killer die wouldn't help them feel better, so why bother? Or, possibly because the deaths occurred 14 years ago, the families had decided to simply move on. They may not have wanted the painful memories of their loved one's murder stirred up again.

For nearly 15 minutes, I sat staring at the brown curtain on the other side of the glass, wondering what was on the other side and what was I going to see. My mind drifted to my family and my life thousands of miles away. I wondered what my wife and my three little boys were doing right then. It was about 5:00 in Minnesota, so they were probably sitting down at the table having supper. My wife would have prepared a nice meal, and my boys would refuse to eat any of it. Instead, they would be tormenting her to fix them pancakes or peanut butter and honey sandwiches with chocolate milk. My wife would lead the family in a prayer before dinner and would probably pray that I would ...

My thoughts of Camille and the boys were interrupted when I noticed movement in the death room. Through the brown curtain, I saw a little flash of white. Someone wearing white had entered the room on the other side of the glass. I pressed my forehead right up against the thin glass and strained to look through the coarsely woven fabric. I focused on the tiny spaces between the weaves in the drape and I saw him.

I identified the distinct shape of a hospital gurney being wheeled into the room. There was a person lying on the gurney and I knew it must be Edward Castro. The figures that had wheeled the gurney into the room took something from the side of the gurney. I couldn't see what it was, but they moved it to the wall on the other side of room. Remembering the execution protocol I had read on the Florida State Web site, I guessed that they must have been feeding the IV tubes through a hole in the wall. The executioner on the other side would then connect those tubes to the poisons that would kill Castro. I watched the shadowy figures move out of my view and continued to attempt to see through the curtain.

Suddenly the curtain opened and I jumped slightly, startled by its quick movement. Before my eyes, lying less then 3 feet in front of me, was the man I had come to see die: the violent, serial killer, Edward Castro. The tension I had experienced ten minutes before, while waiting with the curtain closed, was nothing compared to how I felt now, with the curtain opened and Castro right in front of me.

"Oh no ... oh no ... I can't do this," I thought to myself. "I can't see this ... I am not ready to see this ... this can't be happening ... I want to be at home ... please, let me out! Please let me out!" I don't know what one can do to prepare for an execution, or what one can do to lessen the shock of looking at a man who is about to be killed, but whatever it is, I hadn't done it and wasn't prepared.

I had a flashback to my freshman year in college, when I sat in my dorm room and watched Operation Desert Storm (the Gulf War) escalating before me on television. In the days leading up to the invasion, one news commentator expressed his view that this military action could turn into another Vietnam War, with young men drafted into armed service. I remembered how I had thought to myself, "Cool! I get to watch a war! I might even get to fight in it!"

But when the first videos came in, showing rockets streaking through the night air toward their targets and machine guns ripping off rounds, I announced out loud to my roommates, "I am not ready for this. I can't fight in a war. I am scared, and I don't want to do this." It sounded fun and glamorous when it was just an idea, but when it became a reality, I knew that I was in no way prepared to deal with a war.

I felt exactly the same way sitting in the viewing area that evening. My stomach tightened and I felt sick. My heart beat with an intensity that frightened me. My body was responding both to the imminent death and to its proximity to a threat. Psychologists call this reaction the "fight or flight" instinct. Adrenaline rushes through the body, preparing it for battle or giving it the extra energy to run away from danger. I wanted to run, but I was locked in the chamber, and the homicidal maniac that I had read about was inches away from me.

I noticed that Castro couldn't get to me and I tried to relax a little. He was lying on his back with his arms stretched out. Ace bandages and leather straps restrained him at the wrists. He wore a short-sleeve, white dress shirt that looked many sizes too large for him. The shirt was unbuttoned at the neck. A thin, white sheet covered his body up to the midsection. The sheet was so thin that I could see the thick leather straps that held him to the gurney, beneath it.

Had it not been for the IV tubes in his arms, Castro would have looked like a man restrained to prevent injury to himself. He could have been a psychotic patient who was unstable and needed restraints to keep him from lashing out at himself or others. As it was though, there was one IV tube sticking out of the crook of each arm and he looked helpless rather than threatening.

As in the photos that I had seen of Castro, his head was completely shaved. I was close enough to see the short stubble on his face. I deduced that he had not shaved that day probably because he was thinking that the act was pointless. Castro's neck rested on a blue support that looked like some type of pillow. It looked like the pillow was intended to keep Castro's head immobilized after his death, looking straight up at the ceiling. It didn't look comfortable, but at that point, the dying man's comfort wasn't really an issue.

Castro's right arm, which was so close to where I sat that I could have touched it, if not for the glass between us, was covered in an intricate tattoo. The design was dark green and black, except for a rising (or setting) sun that was blood red. At some point in his life, Castro had sat in some dirty tattoo parlor to have a beautiful design cut into his skin. He had decided to keep the whole design plain except for the rays of the sun, which he must have thought looked better in red. It seemed strange, and a bit haunting, to me that now he was lying on his back with a needle poked through the middle of his beautiful tattoo.

I thought about Castro's tattoo for many weeks after his execution. I spent far too much time wondering if the sun was rising, like a new birth, or setting, like the death of a day.

CHAPTER TWENTY

In just moments, the needle in the middle of Castro's mysterious tattoo would carry poison through his blood and into his heart, ending the man's troubled life. The IV tubing ran from Castro's arms to the gurney, where adhesive tape held it firmly to the side of his deathbed. My eyes followed the tubes from the gurney, away from Castro, and to a 6-inch-square hole in the wall, where they had been fed through the opening in the wall. Beyond our sight, the tubes connected to a bag of saline solution, and the salt-water solution was already flowing into Castro's blood stream.

Presumably, the executioner sat on the other side of that wall, and when signaled, would begin injecting the poisons into the solution running through the killer's veins. The executioner was actually the only person paid, and I had read that he would receive $150 for the killing. The other 11 witnesses and I were all considered volunteers, and I thought that was fair. We sat and watched the show, while the executioner actually did the killing. In a sense, he was the star of the whole, sick opera, and I was just a nauseated chorus member.

Three prison officials stood in the room with Edward Castro, positioned off to my left in a recessed portion of the room that looked about 4 feet square. These were the same men I had seen earlier, in the warden's office. Thinking back to the execution protocol I had read, I concluded that they must be warden, and two officials from the Department of Corrections for the State of Florida. All three men were dressed in sport coats and polyester slacks, and looked anxious. One of the officials had a shaved head and looked remarkably similar to Edward Castro, though I doubted that anyone would point that out to him on this particular day.

On a wall near the opening of the small alcove where the men waited, I could see a switch labeled "ON" and "OFF." The warden's hand hovered near it, and I wondered if this lever, which was out of Castro's view, would deliver the poison to the inmate. Directly in front of me, on the other side of Edward Castro's outstretched body, two large and imposing prison guards stood against the far wall. Both were tall and muscular and held their hands tightly clasped in front of them. Neither man looked like he knew how to smile. Their short haircuts looked military-issue to me, and I sat close enough to see that one of the men wore a United States Marine Corps ring on his right hand. I wondered if he knew that the man on the table before him was a fellow Semper Fi brother?

The guards tried to appear tough, uncompromising, and untouched by the death they were about to witness. But to me they looked unsure of themselves and out of place. They seemed scared and vulnerable; certainly not as vulnerable as the man 2 feet in front of them did, but vulnerable nevertheless. Although they tried not to let it show, they must have felt uncomfortable being on display in front of all the witnesses.

I felt sorry for them.

I was sorry to see that they were trying so hard to convey a presence of masculinity and strength that it instead made them appear frail. I wondered, as I sat staring at them staring at me, if they really didn't want the job they were now performing. Maybe some informal code among prison guards required them to participate in executions. Or perhaps the men had volunteered, as I had. Whatever brought them to that room with the dying Edward Castro, it was clear to me that they didn't want to be there.

I noticed that neither of these two men ever actually looked at Castro. They were not required to observe his execution. That was my job. Their role was to look "in control" of the situation, and they didn't. I began to wonder if I was going to fail at my task that night, too.

Shifting my gaze from the two guards, I saw a slender, well-dressed man on the far right side of the room. He looked about 35 years old and wore a very stylish suit that would have been more appropriate for a dance club than an execution chamber. I imagined him wearing that outfit at a party, getting compliments from women he met there. He would graciously accept the praise, but would probably not mention that he bought the suit to wear while performing executions.

From the time that the curtain opened until moments before I left the room, this man remained on the telephone that hung on the wall at Castro's feet. Several days before, I had read that a phone line to the Governor's Office must be open at all times in the execution room. Also nearby will be a cell phone with "a fully charged battery," as it is spelled out in the Official Execution Protocol. I then realized that less than 6 feet away from me, a prison employee was currently talking with Florida Governor Jeb Bush, the brother of the man who would win the United States Presidential Election (by most accounts) a few days later.

In a soft voice, and with his hand covering his mouth to prevent others from listening in on the conversation, the sharply-dressed man continued talking with the governor. Governor Jeb Bush would give the final authorization for the execution to proceed and could, with a single word, stop the entire process. The telephone remained connected to the Governor's office in the event that he decided, at the last possible moment, to grant a stay of execution, or to commute the sentence altogether and allow Edward Castro to live the rest of his painful life behind prison bars.

I looked back at the two muscular prison guards standing next to Castro. Behind them, a black curtain hung from the ceiling and stopped about 2 feet above the floor. I peered at that space between the floor and the bottom hem of the curtain and saw a black, rubber floor mat which is mounted beneath an electric chair. This small, curtained-off area, which couldn't have been more than 8 feet in front of me, covered the electric chair for the State of Florida. The feet of dozens of condemned men had rested on that same rubber mat, as an electrical current fried their brains. And there I sat, in the same room, separated from this device by only a thin piece of Plexiglas.

Shaken, I redirected my stare away from the electric chair and back to the man on the gurney. From the moment that the curtain had opened, providing an unobstructed view of Edward Castro, the feeling in the room became tense. My heart rate had been steadily increasing over the last six days leading up to this very moment. Each time I looked at some clock and counted down the hours until the execution, my heart would noticeably speed up. As the day of the execution had drawn closer, my breath had begun to come in short, hard gasps like my body was struggling to suck oxygen from thin air. It felt like I was about to watch someone being killed.

"I can't do this, I can't do this, I can't do this, I can't do this," I kept telling myself over and over again. I was about to stand up and leave … to run out of the room, past the prison fences to my rental car. I wanted to get away from the whole scene while I still felt innocent and clean.

I quickly glanced around the room and noted again that the reinforced metal door we had all entered through was now closed, locked and guarded. The guard watched me as I scanned the room for an exit, as though he knew what I was thinking. I interpreted the expression on his face to read, "You got yourself into this, now it's time to see it through."

At that moment I hated myself. I was afraid of what I was going to see, but I was there and I had to do it. I was going to force myself to watch this execution happen. I reluctantly returned my gaze to the window in front of me, where I sat face to face with Edward Castro.

The man on the gurney seemed calm, which surprised me. I expected an inmate going to his death to be angry and fighting. But Castro appeared very relaxed. Perhaps he had accepted his death, which he himself had hurried along by firing his lawyers earlier in the year. Or maybe the Valium injection he had been given earlier facilitated a calm, but lucid, state.

Castro scanned the group of witnesses, including me, and seemed to look for someone in particular. He found that person sitting in the front row, in the last chair on the left. I now knew why witnesses had been directed not to sit in that chair. That spot had been reserved for the man seated there now; the man who Castro first looked to as soon as the curtain opened. The plain-looking, middle-aged man looked like a parent who had come to the school principal's office to see his favorite son that has just gotten into trouble.

Castro made eye contact with the man within a second of the curtain opening and gave him a wide smile. The man at the end of the row returned a more reserved smile to the inmate before him. Castro's smile made him appear embarrassed and humble, and he quickly looked away from the man, starring up at the bright ceiling lights. I wondered if we had just seen a moment of shame on the face of this hardened criminal.

Castro's smile seemed friendly and I could see how his victims found him charming. There are some people whose faces look like they were just born to smile. Castro was one of them. And then there are others whose faces seemed to never permit a smile. Interestingly, the prison warden, who stood immediately behind Castro and physically resembled the killer, was one of the latter.

After a few seconds, Castro again looked at the man sitting two seats away from me. He smiled again and nodded his head, as if saying, "Hello." Castro made eye contact with the observer and held it for about ten seconds, which is a long time to stare directly into someone's eyes without being able to speak with him. I wondered who this man, with an obvious connection to the killer, was?

He was probably not a close relative, since Castro was Latino and this gentleman sitting near me looked Caucasian. Considering Castro's obvious attachment to the man, it also seemed unlikely that he was a family member of one of Castro's victims. However, one can't rule that out. I had recently read an account of a rapist and murderer who befriended the parents of the woman he brutalized and killed. While on death row, the victim's family forgave their daughter's killer, adopting the man, in a sense, and worked to free him. When the killer was ultimately executed, the victim's family told the media that they felt as if they had lost a son.

The reaction of that poor woman's parents amazed me. While I study human behavior for a living, and have witnessed unusual bonds and attachments between people many times, I failed to understand these people. How could they have looked at her killer and seen anything other than the man who slit their daughter's throat as she begged for her life?

But with that in mind, I considered the possibility that this might be one of those rare cases. I looked from Castro to his acquaintance sitting near me. Maybe this poor, grieving man, in his desperation and loneliness, clung to the killer who took his loved one's life. But the man didn't look like he was grieving. He simply looked calm and reassuring. Then it occurred to me ... the man was probably a priest or minister, there to comfort Castro during his final minutes.

After breaking eye contact with the man for a second time, Castro looked back up at the ceiling lights and simply waited. I wondered what he was thinking about. Had it occurred to him, when he first lay on the gurney minutes before, that he would never climb off it? In fact, did he know that he would leave the gurney as a corpse? As he stared straight ahead, did he acknowledge to himself that he would never again see ceiling panels, or ceiling lights, or the sparkly, plastic covers over them? He was going to die. He wasn't going to see anything again. His life was over. Did he think about that as he lay there with his arms outstretched, waiting?

The prison officials and guards in the death chamber remained quiet and stared at the floor. The warden, and his two companions in the recessed area to the left, whispered to one another briefly. Otherwise, nobody in the death chamber spoke. Everyone seemed to be nervously waiting for something.

After a couple of minutes, the warden reached over to the switch on the wall next to him and threw it toward the top position that was clearly labeled "On." I wondered if this was it ... if this action turned on the poisons? But then I heard the slight hum, like that of my stereo speakers powering up. Evidently the switch controlled the microphone that hung over Castro's gurney, not the syringes behind the wall. The warden then spoke the only words that I heard him say that day, asking Castro, "Do you have a final statement to make?"

Castro looked toward the microphone hanging from the ceiling over his head. He appeared nervous, but in control. In that mood, the multiple murderer, Edward Castro, used his final breaths to speak these final words. "I would like to thank my family and everyone, who has prayed for me and kept me in their prayers," he began. "I would like to thank my spiritual advisor, Dan," he continued, and then paused to look over at the man in the last seat on the left of the front row. Again, Castro smiled and nodded at him. He then looked back at the ceiling, and said, "I ask God to forgive you for what you are about to do to me. Forgive them ... um ... they know not what they do."

My breath quickened. I was enraged! How dare he compare himself to Jesus dying on the cross! As he was being crucified, Jesus had uttered the same line, "Father, forgive them, they know not what they do." Castro's arms were outstretched, like Christ's were at the time of his death, and the gurney resembled a cross, with its arm planks extended outward. True, Castro was dying at the hands of a government trying to appease its people, just as Christ did, but the similarities ended there. One man was perfect and lived his life without malice or any harm to others. The other man killed people, and I believed he enjoyed killing people. They were not the same, and Castro's comparison bordered on delusion.

Castro continued with his statement, "I would like to apologize to the victims' families. And, again, thanks to everyone for keeping me in their prayers and for giving me your love and support ... That's it." With that, he was finished. He had said all he had to say.

Until I heard Castro's final statement, I had never become angry with the man, even though I knew what he had done. But I was enraged when I heard his words, "I would like to apologize to the families of the victims." That's it? Not even "my victims?" He passively referred to the men he brutally butchered to death as "the victims." In his final opportunity to make amends and confess his murders to us, he still did not take responsibility for the crimes he had committed. I got the sense that he felt obligated to mention the people he had killed, but his apology sounded weak and without feeling.

This man was the real thing.

He was a killer.

Edward Castro might have been sorry about the murders, but I didn't think he was sorry for the pain it caused his victims or their families. It sounded to me like he was sorry that he got caught. He was sorry that things turned out the way they did. Sure, Castro was remorseful, but only because of the difficulty it caused for him, not because of his actions. He was sorry for what was about to happen to him, but not sorry for what he did that got him into that execution chamber in the first place.

Castro was a classic sociopath.

He was a hardened and emotionally-calloused murderer, beyond social redemption or rehabilitation. Castro was a killer, and I knew that if he were on the street he would kill again. I have talked with killers before, but I had never before sat that close to evil, and I recognized it.

I feared it.

I was afraid of Edward Castro.

Castro was held down with straps and was surrounded by guards who could have broken a common man in half, and yet I was afraid of him. I was afraid of what he was, and what he could do to me. Rationally, I knew it was impossible, but I feared that somehow, at that moment, he could kill me.

I imagined meeting Castro outside the prison, and could only see myself as his victim. What if he was waiting in the back seat of my car? Or hiding in the closet of my home? Or waiting near the front door of my house? He would kill me. He was a killer and I could have been one of his victims. He would do it for money, or for my car, or for some other immediate gratification. But he would kill me, or anyone else, if he were given the chance.

At first, I might fear that he was going to kill me, but then I'd dismiss the idea. No one really thinks it will ever happen to them. Castro, as a predator, would sense my fear and lull me into passivity, just as he did to Jason Miller, his first known victim in Florida. He would get me to relax and then catch me off guard. He would dive on me and knock me to the ground, just as he did with Miller and Carter.

If Castro attacked me, he would choke me until I was nearly unconscious, as he did with his final victim. But then he would stop, like he did with Carter and Williams, the teenager who almost became a murder victim. Because he would stop choking me, I would think I had been spared.

But then I would see him pick up a sharp knife and show it to me. I would hear him say, as he always did to his victims, "You ready for this, man? You are already dead, man. You might as well let it happen. Don't fight it, it's gonna happen. Just take it like a man."

Then he would start stabbing me in my chest and I would feel the metal rip into my virgin flesh. I would try to fight, and I would be stabbed in my hands and arms. Later, the medical examiner would refer to these as "defensive wounds" in his autopsy report.

The lack of oxygen to my brain, caused by the choking, would make me weak. My throat would burn with pain from where he had throttled me moments before. But my attention would shift to the unimaginable pain in my chest and lungs.

Stab wounds to the heart normally don't produce much blood outside the victim, contrary to popular belief. The heart generally stops beating when pierced with a knife, and, therefore, very little blood comes out. Some blood, however, would leak into my lungs and I would cough uncontrollably trying to expel the fluid from my airway. But I wouldn't have the strength to cough hard enough.

Castro would be sitting next to me, like some predators do after they have delivered their deadly bite. He would be waiting for me to die. He would look at my kicking feet and struggled breathing, but he wouldn't help me. I would think of my family, in my final moments. In my mind, I would see Camille and I would note the ways I could have been a better husband for her. I would be thinking of my three, wonderful little boys, and how they loved to wrestle with me, and kiss me, and hug me. Who would provide for them? Will they be OK?

Soon, I would begin to feel cold, first in my hands and feet, but eventually throughout my entire body. After a few more moments, I would feel lightheaded and dizzy, detached and confused. Then I would drift away. The years and years of school, the unrealized hopes and desires would all be gone. The man who loved his family more than life would never see them again. Everything would be gone.

Castro would take all of that from me, if he had the chance, and he would not feel sorrow for my loss for even a second. Castro was the real thing, and he was exactly what each of us fears the most. He was a horrifying murderer who would rip you to pieces and only regret that he was caught doing it.

Castro was a cold-blooded killer and I was about to watch him die.

———

After he made his final statement, he looked toward the ceiling again and, this time, closed his eyes. The movement was so sudden that I wondered if he had just died quickly, without my noticing how it happened. The large, red digital clock on the wall read 6:01 and Castro was lying perfectly still, with his eyes closed. I glanced at the other witnesses wondering if somehow I had just missed something. They were all still staring at the man and no one returned my look.

I stared hard at Castro for a few moments. He was less than a yard away from me, and I could see his eyelids flutter and his chest move in and out slowly as he breathed. He was still alive.

No stay of execution was granted.

The Supreme Court of the United States didn't intervene on behalf of Edward Castro.

The Pope of the Roman Catholic Church, who had done so in the past for other killers, did not ask for clemency for this condemned man.

Castro wasn't wealthy; so President Bill Clinton didn't pardon him.

There would be no last-minute appeals.

The final moment had arrived, and the execution of Edward Castro began.

On the other side of the wall in front of me, out of my view, the executioner had been signaled to begin. Following protocol, he picked up the syringe marked #1, held the IV tube, and injected the entire volume of sodium pentothal into the saline solution already flowing into Edward Castro's body. He immediately followed that injection with a second one of sodium pentothal, in the syringe marked #2. Finally, he administered a third syringe of saline solution, intended to flush out the line and make sure that there were no clogs or kinks, to obstruct the lethal doses of poison entering Castro's body.

Back on our side of the wall, the drugs hit Edward Castro's arms. His eyes jerked open and his muscular body tensed.

I recalled a feeling I had experienced a month before the execution, when I was hospitalized for a minor medical procedure. General anesthetic was given to me through an IV line, just like those sticking out of Castro's arms. I could not feel the saline solution going into my body, but when the physician injected the drug that would render me unconscious, I could feel it going into my veins. The anesthetic itched and burned slightly as it flowed into my body. The fluid felt cold as it moved down my arms. While this lasted only 20 to 30 seconds, until I passed out, I clearly remember it. I felt the drug going into me.

And so did Edward Castro.

His eyes jerked open and a look of pained concentration came over his face. Without moving his head, he looked around the room and continued to grimace slightly. His brow furrowed and his face scrunched up a bit.

Castro looked concerned. Not scared or alarmed, but concerned.

His body shifted under the leather straps and his restrained arms twisted slightly as the near lethal dose of anesthetic raced through his arms toward his heart. The dying man looked around the room, and then at his body, and he began to breathe more heavily.

So did I.

His head barely moved, but his eyes looked like black bugs that had been sprayed with Raid. They writhed and scrambled for cover, but to no avail. They were already dead ... they just hadn't accepted it yet. Castro knew he was dying and, for the first time since I had seen him, he looked like he was about to panic.

On the other side of the wall, the final five syringes were pushed into the IV tubing in rapid succession. The first and second of the five final syringes were filled with a drug called pancuronium bromide, which paralyzed his muscles. With this drug, his taut muscular tissue couldn't respond to voluntary movement and the killer became completely paralyzed. The executioner followed these with a syringe full of saline solution, and then a fatal dose of the drug potassium chloride, which would stop his heart. Finally, another syringe of saline was pushed into his IV line and we all waited. The executioner, the guards, the witnesses, the doctors, the warden, the Governor, Castro, and me, all waited for him to die.

He began to noticeably relax and I began to noticeably tighten.

Edward Castro was dying.

I could hardly believe it—I was watching a man die.

His eyes were still open and darting around the room.

He then lifted his chin up slightly and sharply exhaled.

Castro gasped and arched his back, trying to suck in as much air as possible. He looked as if he were trying to suppress a yawn by keeping his mouth closed. His lips began to tremble slightly, as did his whole body.

His body jerked slightly and Castro inhaled a breath of air so large that I thought that there was no way he could keep it in without rupturing his lungs. I didn't know if the enormous breath was due to the drugs, or if Castro was fighting to stay alive. But the breath was far too deep to be considered normal.

And he didn't exhale that breath.

It looked to me like he couldn't. He lay there, with his eyes open, looking around for a few seconds, and couldn't exhale the massive amount of air he had just drawn in. His back arched again, this time more sharply, and his whole body shook for just a moment. His mouth opened and trembled and he began to blink his eyes. Gradually, the blinking of his eyes became slower until, after one blink, his eyes didn't open. Inside his body, Castro's muscles became paralyzed. He could not move at all, even if he were awake. At the same time, a drug headed toward his heart and would invade the vital organ and stop its beating. If he were awake, he would have incredible chest pains, just like his victims had, and would feel as if he were having a heart attack.

But Castro was asleep. Could he feel any pain? What was he thinking? Did he know that, at that second, he was dying?

I sat next to this perfectly healthy man, and stared into his face, waiting for him to breathe, or move, or open his eyes.

But he didn't.

Along with 11 other witnesses, I sat watching a man die and there was nothing I could do about it. Outside the building, the two morticians stood next to the white hearse, smoking cigarettes and waiting for it to all be over.

I kept staring at Castro's face, feeling my own heart racing nearly out of control in my tightening chest. He didn't move, even a twitch, for three or four minutes. I wondered if he was dead.

How would I know if he was dead?

If Castro was dead, why was I still sitting there? How long would they leave me in there with him? What if he was still alive? Could he feel anything?

The whole scene, the actors and all the stage props did not seem real to me. It could not be happening.

After about six minutes of staring into his blank face and slightly open mouth, Castro's lips began to turn blue. His face took on a light gray color and his lips and eyelids became a dark purple color.

Edward Castro was dead.

I had watched him die.

By serving as a witness, I had aided in the process of killing a man.

CHAPTER TWENTY-ONE

The man on the phone with the Governor stood perfectly still with the phone to his ear, silently staring at the floor. Not one of the guards or prison officials in the room looked at Castro, who was obviously the center of attention. They glanced at their shoes, at their fingernails, at me, at the other witnesses or at the ceiling. They looked at everything else in the room but the dead man we all came to see.

I made eye contact with one of the two barrel-chested guards, the one with the U.S. Marine Corps ring, and stared at him. His head remained motionless and he looked back at me. Obviously, I couldn't know what he was thinking, but I wondered if he was as confused and scared as I was. I sensed that my staring was annoying him, so I glanced back at the dead man, the executed serial killer.

Castro's face looked less ashen than it had appeared seconds before, but that might have been my imagination. I was literally growing sick of looking at the dead Edward Castro and I wondered how long I would have to sit there "witnessing" his death. I was too afraid to look around the room at the other witnesses. I don't know why, but I was afraid of them, too. Yet I needed to know if they wanted this to be over as much as I did.

Why were we still sitting with this dead man? Was everyone waiting for me to stand up and exit the room? Did I miss something?

At 6:15, a middle-aged physician, in a white lab coat, came out from behind the wall near the two burly guards. He was Caucasian, with graying hair and a mustache. He wore glasses and had a stethoscope around his sun-wrinkled neck. I watched the doctor quickly walk around Castro (I couldn't yet think of Castro as a "body.") and step right in front of me. He had to turn sideways and shuffle his feet to get between Castro's outstretched hand and the thin window that my face was pressed up against.

The physician had his back to me but I could see him begin to unbutton Castro's white dress shirt. I marveled at the calm he exhibited. Perhaps death frightened me more than it frightened this man. I would have been more nervous around Castro. But he appeared to be totally at ease in his examination of the man.

Earlier, I had wondered why Castro did not wear the bright orange jumpsuit to his execution that inmates on death row are required to wear. The medical exam now answered my question. The orange jumpsuits did not have buttons that could be undone to allow a stethoscope to be applied to the bare chest of the prisoner, which was exactly what the physician was doing.

The physician placed the stethoscope on several different locations on Castro's chest and listened at each one. After only about ten to 15 seconds of listening, and a total of about 30 seconds with "the patient," the exam was complete. I was shocked that he could so quickly determine that the man was dead. The physician removed his stethoscope and walked back behind the wall. Instantly, another doctor appeared from behind the wall. This man appeared to be about ten years older than the first doctor, and this made him look more distinguished than his predecessor.

The second doctor approached Castro, lifted the inmate's eyelids and looked at his eyeballs, to determine if any brain activity was present. If the pupil of the eye contracts when the eye is exposed to light, then there is still activity in the brain and the "executed" man is still alive. This can often happen, since oxygenated blood can remain in the brain for several minutes after the heart stops beating. After the heart stops, the patient can still be "alive" until the cells in the brain use up the last of the oxygen in the blood. The first physician didn't check this, and falsely assumed that Castro was dead because he couldn't hear a heart beat.

The second, and more thorough, exam continued. After allowing Castro's eyes to close, the physician then listened for breath by putting his ear next to Castro's nose and slightly open mouth. I would have been terrified to place my face that close to Castro. But the physician had likely seen many inmates die this way, and he no doubt trusted the drugs more than I did.

After listening near Castro's blue lips for five to ten seconds, he put his hands on the man's chest to feel for movement. Finding that it was still, he then listened with his own stethoscope for nearly 30 seconds. This seemed like an eternity compared to the length of time the first doctor listened.

He then removed the stethoscope from Castro's chest and looking toward the man on the phone, said, "He's done; 6:16 p.m.; he's dead." He then walked back behind the wall and out of my sight.

Edward Castro was dead.

I had just watched the execution of a murderer.

I had just watched the execution of a person.

The man on the phone with the Governor's office said something into the phone, but all I caught were the words "6:16 p.m." and "dead." He hung up the telephone and took out a pen from the pocket of his expensive suit. I watched him make a note on a three-by-five index card, before he took two steps forward and stood next to Castro's feet. Without looking directly at the witnesses, he read from the card, "The sentence of death against Edward Castro by the State of Florida has been carried out at 6:16 p.m. Thank you for your service, please exit the room immediately."

I saw Edward Castro for the last time as the Warden quickly closed the brown curtain, covering the glass in front of me.

CHAPTER TWENTY-TWO

Numbly, I stood with the other witnesses and began to slowly shuffle out of the room. The group of reporters sitting in the last row of chairs stared at each of us, but I was the only person staring back at them. One or two looked at me and then jotted something down on their notebooks. I didn't care. They could have said anything they wanted to me or about me ... I just didn't care.

Outside the death house, the afternoon had turned into evening and it was now dark. I learned later that somewhere outside the fence of the prison, mourners, protesters, and the family of Edward Castro were praying and holding a candlelight vigil. Some of the protesters were specifically opposed to Castro's execution because of his childhood trauma and severe mental problems, while others were opposed to any execution. They prayed and stared at their watches. There were tears and hugs and a general feeling of anger, hopelessness and despair. While I didn't even know they were there, that night I felt exactly the same way these people did.

I stood silently with the other witnesses, staring at the ground. No one made a sound. If I were asked a question, I doubt I could have said anything at all. I was about to begin the second worst night of my life.

The worst night of my young life happened seven years earlier. We had been married a few months when, one day at Wal-Mart, I found myself staring and smiling at an unknown woman's baby. The baby smiled back at me and I was hooked. My wife commented that I looked "baby hungry" and within a month or so she was pregnant.

Camille and I bought books on babies, childbirth, and infant development. Every day we looked at one of the guides to see what the baby in her womb was doing that day. We would find that today our baby would have a heartbeat or today our baby had fingers or today our baby had eyes. We were the most excited parents on the planet.

In October 1993, two months into the pregnancy, my wife started bleeding. We called our doctor right away, and then both of our mothers, and heard from all three that it was probably nothing that bed rest couldn't cure. A day later she began cramping and bleeding more heavily. We called our doctor at his home at midnight and he asked my wife about her symptoms. Camille described what was happening to her body. And then he told her what we were afraid to hear; she was probably having a miscarriage.

I could not accept that this death had to happen. For the next eight hours we both cried and prayed as our baby was dying inside Camille. I was angry with God, the doctor, myself, and everyone else I could think of. Someone, somewhere could stop it and save my baby but I didn't know who and I didn't know how to find him. By morning, we had lost our first baby and I had nearly lost my faith in God and myself. Standing there in the prison yard after the execution, I felt the same anger and hopelessness that I had seven years before.

Detached, I noticed my emotions slowly slipping out of my control. My mind felt like a fast-moving car on an impossibly icy road. When the wheels lose traction, there is little the driver can do to control the dangerous machine. He can try turning the steering wheel into the skid, but that doesn't always stop the impending doom. Sometimes you have to simply wait for the ride to be over. You know the crash is coming and all you can do is wait for it. I felt a crash coming and I couldn't prevent it.

I couldn't believe that our government had the right to do to someone what I had just seen done. And there was nothing that I could do about it. I could have stood up during the execution and pounded on the glass, but I would have simply been removed from the chamber and another witness would have taken my place. The government was going to kill the man, with or without my presence. This scared me more than anything else did at that moment. I felt weak and powerless. For some confusing reason, I feared that I would do something to cause my own execution, like Edward Castro had done, and there was nothing that I could do about it. I felt out of control.

We were quickly loaded back into the van for the short drive to the warden's office. None of us spoke or even looked at each other for more than a passing second. I stared at other witnesses until they looked up at me and then we both quickly avoided eye contact. We were acting guilty. Even those that had watched executions before were acting guilty, as if they had just been caught doing something wrong and were ashamed of themselves for their moment of weakness.

We were dropped off at the warden's office and we all entered the poorly-lit brick building. We were led into the reception area of the office; the same place I had earlier mistakenly thought the woman with the hands-free telephone was speaking to me. We stood in a loosely organized group and a prison administrator that I had not seen before quietly thanked us for our service. He then asked us if anyone would like to speak with a counselor.

I felt horribly confused and sure that I was going to die. My mouth was as dry as burnt cotton and I fought to control my shaking hands. I had never felt this way before. I felt, in many ways, like someone else. I had changed into some unknown man, and found that my mind and body didn't quite fit me right anymore. I had died a painful and violent death in the preceding minutes and a confused version of me emerged from the death house that night.

I stood with everyone else in the warden's office but I ignored the meaningless chatter of the other witnesses. I felt my mind slipping and the only thing I could think about was trying not to scream and fall to the ground in front of the others.

I thought of something a psychologist, and friend of mine, once told me. He said that extreme stress could produce altered states of consciousness. These "altered states" can make us believe things that aren't real. It can make us see things that aren't there. I had seen something so unreal in that execution that my mind was beginning to lose its ability to think clearly.

I felt like a disgustingly ugly insect going through a violently short metamorphosis. My mind and body were being ripped out of control and I felt bugs crawling on my skin. I couldn't get enough air into my lungs and they began to feel like they had thick hair growing inside them.

While I hadn't noticed it earlier, one of the grief counselors, available to talk with us should we became confused or emotionally troubled after watching the killing, looked disturbingly sexy to me. She leaned against the wall in a white blouse that looked just like the one Edward Castro had worn a few minutes earlier. All I could think of was touching her beautiful face before it turned purple and blue like Castro's did. My mind was racing back and forth between images of lust, passion and death.

I had to get out. If I stayed in the now spinning room, I would be sick and vomit all over the place. I had to get out of the prison complex immediately and away from the death.

"Can I go now?" I asked loudly, and to no one in particular. I felt that the whole world was dying and I was the only person who recognized it.

A guard that I had not seen before answered me, from behind the receptionist's desk, "Yes, and thank you all for your help. You are free to go."

When I walked out the door, my friend, David, followed me. "You OK, Doc?" he asked me in his soothing voice.

I hated that he called me "Doc." I hated this man. He made me sick and I couldn't get far enough away from him. I also wanted to hug him passionately and kiss him firmly on the cheek as hard as I could, and then smash him under the wheels of my rental car. I hated him.

In a deceptively calm voice, I answered politely, "Yeah, I'm fine." But I knew I was lying. I was not fine at all. I was dying. I might, at any second, turn into smoke, drift up into the air and never be seen again. I might even be dead right now … I wasn't sure. Everyone in the world would miss me and cry and cry and cry, but I would be dead, dead, dead and there would be nothing anybody could do to save me.

"The first time is always the hardest," he told me, as we walked toward our cars, "but you'll be OK You're a smart guy." Smart people apparently deal well with watching the execution of others.

I didn't say it, but I thought to myself, "I guess I'm not that smart because I am very far from OK" In fact, I was decidedly *not* OK and I couldn't see how I might ever get OK again. I had lost something in that execution chamber. I didn't know what it was, but I had lost it and I feared that I would never be the same.

David and I wordlessly parted company forever and I got into my cheap rental car. For a second I couldn't remember how to start a car. You had to put something in the ignition … keys. I needed keys. Where were they? I found the keys in a pocket. I had my keys. OK, relax.

I'M DYING! DEAR GOD, HELP ME, I'M DYING!

"Relax, put the key into the ignition," I told myself, "and turn the key to start the car." I thought about when the car was built. Sometime within the last year, an automobile assembly line worker put this ignition into this very car. I wondered if they have ever seen someone die like I just had. Up close. And a healthy person, too. Up close. Front row seat. Front row seats at concerts are more expensive because the show is better when you are closer to the stage. I had had a very "expensive" ticket to this event.

My heart was going to stop.

My blood was getting heavy and thick.

I was not going to make it out of the prison yard alive.

I started the car and drove out of the prison toward the small town of Starke. I passed church after church and continued to drive toward town. I didn't know where I was going but I had to get there quickly. I looked down at my speedometer and saw that I was driving only about 30 mph. The speed limit on this road was 55, but I was afraid of exceeding it so I drove slowly. Very, very slowly.

I was dying and I couldn't breathe anymore.

Then I remembered that one could get a ticket for driving too slowly. I immediately sped up to 50 and wondered if that was the right speed. "Fifty might be too slow, too. But what if the speed limit changes to 45? I'll be speeding! What if in Florida you are supposed to go exactly 55 in a 55 mph zone? What if I get pulled over, and then because I am acting so strangely the cop might get nervous and draw his gun and shoot me through the head? I would hear an explosion and the bullet would rip a hole through my skull and tear parts of my brain out and I would kick and struggle as my blood squirted out of my head."

I started crying while driving the car. I didn't want to die. I love my family. I didn't want to die without seeing them.

I somehow made it to Starke and drove to a Wal-Mart. I walked into the discount store determined to buy something to make myself feel better. I didn't know if it would be a gun or a knife, but there had to be relief in there somewhere. As I passed the electronics section I saw what I needed. It cost $19.96 but there was one almost like it for $21.96. I couldn't decide which one to buy. I stood there staring at them both. Each time I picked one up, the other looked better and I changed my mind. For ten minutes, I stood staring at them both and eventually decided on one over the other, though I don't remember which. I picked out all the accessories I needed to make the thing work and I proceeded to the checkout line.

The cashier who rang up my purchases must have been at least 65 or 70 years old. She had skin that looked like she had found it in the trunk of a used car and decided to half-heartedly staple it to her face. It hung down in places and was wrinkled beyond recognition. Her teeth were real, I could tell, because the few that she had were black and misshapen. The woman's voice sounded like it came from the grave and I knew that she must have smoked at least 12 packs of cigarettes a day. I was strongly aroused and deeply sexually attracted to her. I wanted her even more than I wanted the counselor at the prison, which seemed like years ago.

Castro had combined sex and death in his killings. Was that the reason for my sudden sexual excitement for any woman that I met that evening? Did the killing I had just taken part in provoke me erotically? Was this how Castro felt when he made the decision to kill each of his victims? Maybe he wasn't gay, but was sexually turned on by contemplating killing the men that he attacked.

Other killers had been known to mix sex and death. In 1998, Karla Faye Tucker was electrocuted by the state of Texas for killing two people with a pickax. Upon her arrest, she stated that killing them was the most erotic and intense sexual event of her life. She likened slamming the point of the pick into her victim's skull to one long, continuous orgasm. It horrified me to imagine it, as I stood there at Wal-Mart, but did my arousal and sexual attraction to this old woman stem from the killing that I had just taken part in?

The sociologist inside me surfaced briefly. "No," I decided firmly. My intense desires were more of a longing for solace than for sex. I was so disturbed and frightened at what I had done that I sought solace, in the form of sex and physical reassurance, from anyone I could find. I was attracted to whoever I thought could make me feel secure and I chose women that either reminded me of my wife, like the short, blonde counselor in the prison, or who looked comforting and grandmotherly, like the Wal-Mart cashier. I wanted relief from the stress of the killing I had just watched. I knew that my arousal was different than the sexual excitement that those killers felt during their attacks.

The wrinkled employee rang up my purchase and handed me the bag. I walked out of the store into the dark parking lot and suddenly couldn't remember where I had parked my car. Worse, I couldn't even remember what kind of car it was. I knew that the car wasn't white, but that was about all I could remember about the car I drove.

I slowly walked up and down the aisles of the parking lot, carrying what I had purchased in a blue, plastic Wal-Mart bag, staring at the cars one by one. Periodically, I stopped where I was and thought about the execution. I would stand in the parking lot for an unknown length of time, thinking about what I had seen moments before, until I remembered that I was looking for my car. At other times, I simply forgot to keep walking. I stopped next to a car that looked familiar. Then I remembered that mine had a sticker on the back, displaying the name of the rental agency, and so I looked to see if this car had a sticker.

There was no sticker, but what I did find was disturbing. On the car was a bright yellow, Florida license plate. That alone wasn't unusual, but this license plate bore the crayon-drawn images of two children. Further, the words "CHOOSE LIFE" were written across the top on the license plate, where normally the state slogan, "Sunshine State" would have been.

Choose life.

Imagine that. Choose life.

In the Wal-Mart parking lot I stared at the happy, bright yellow "Choose Life" license plate and started laughing out loud. Choose life. That's funny. Choose life. Choose it.

Waiter-	Sir, may I take your order?
Gentleman-	Yes, please. I believe I'll choose life. I would like that with the sauce on the side and the rice pilaf rather than the baked potato.
Waiter-	Very good choice, sir. You will be glad you chose life. Ma'am for you?
Ma'am-	No life for me tonight. I would rather choose death. Don't put anything on it. Just bring me the death.
Waiter-	Of course, ma'am. It is your choice.

A couple of weeks later, when I was back home in Minnesota, I read a newspaper article on the subject of pro-life, anti-abortion license plates in various states. It was then that I learned that Florida indeed had such a state-issued plate like the one that I imagined I had seen. I literally thought that I was hallucinating, but it turned out that I actually saw that license plate in the parking lot of the Wal-Mart after I watched an execution.

Somehow I found my car among all the others, and sat inside fumbling with my new purchase. I put in the required items, locked my car door, reclined the seat all the way back, and began talking out loud into my new tape recorder. I had to speak, but I didn't trust myself to talk with another human being. I didn't know what I might say or do, so talking into a tape recorder seemed safer. I sat there and talked into the tiny microphone, recording everything that was on my mind that evening.

From time to time, I checked the car doors, to make sure they were still locked. I didn't feel safe. I killed a murderer, yet I didn't feel any safer now than I had before his death.

In the parking lot of Wal-Mart, I talked into the tape recorder for nearly an hour. People came and went around me, and could see me in my car. I wondered what they thought I was doing there, reclined back in my car seat, in a suit and tie, talking into a black device. But I didn't care. If I didn't talk I was going to explode, and that would look a lot more ridiculous than what I was currently doing. I still have the tape I made that night, but I have never listened to it. I often pick it up and look at it, but I still can't bring myself to listen to what I was thinking during that hour.

I could have talked for hours, filling blank tape after blank tape. But I stopped because I was suddenly starving. I had never been that hungry in my life and I was angry for not eating more at the food orgy sponsored by the prison. I should have eaten everything I could and then stuffed my pockets full of food for later. I was so hungry that I thought I was going to starve to death within the minute if I didn't get food inside me right away. I drove out of the parking lot and pulled into the first fast-food place I saw, a fish and chips restaurant. I took off my suit coat and walked into the restaurant.

At the counter, a teenage, African American girl stood working the cash register. Behind her was another girl, who looked almost exactly like the first, stocking ketchup packets into a dispenser. In the back of the kitchen, I could see two African American men, both in their mid-20s, and a sweaty, African American manager in his late 30s. Standing next to the counter, waiting for her order, was a seriously overweight woman, also African American, perhaps in her late 30s. She had stared at me from the moment I came into the restaurant and I quickly noticed that I was the only non-African American person in the entire restaurant.

I looked up at the menu above the counter and picked out a platter with lots of food on it, and as I approached the counter, the girl by the cash register said, "Can I help you?" She spoke in the most neutral and emotionless tone possible.

I opened my mouth to speak, intending to tell her that I wanted the No. 3 platter, with cole slaw, extra shrimp, two desserts and an extra large Coke, half diet and half regular. But what came out was, "Yeah ... um ... I just watched a guy die. I just watched them execute a man, so I'm ... uh...."

Whatever the fast food worker was expecting to hear from me, that wasn't it.

She stepped back and looked at me like I had just claimed that I was about to give birth to a live snake. I stared back at her and her shocked disbelief turned to wonder. "You mean at the prison, you did? You were just there?"

"Yeah, I just watched a guy get executed." I stammered. "They just executed a killer and I watched it happen."

The girl's twin turned around and the manager came over to see what was going on. The large woman waiting for her food jumped into the conversation, "You for real?"

she asked me. I nodded. "Why'd you do that?" she wanted to know. "I couldn't never do that. Sit there and watch somebody die? I couldn't do that. I mean I think they should do it and everything, but I don't want to watch it."

It bothered me that she said she supported executions, but that she could never watch one herself. I didn't ask her to elaborate on that statement.

For the first time I wondered, "How could someone be in favor of the death penalty and not be willing to watch it carried out?" Wasn't that like saying, "I'm in favor of democracy, but I think voting is disgusting and I could never bring myself to do it?" It seemed to me that you either support it, and you are willing to help execute someone, or you don't.

It didn't seem possible to me that one could be in favor of the death penalty but not be willing to take part in an execution. I had just served as a witness, representing the people of the state of Florida. When the execution was complete, the warden's assistant in the flashy suit read that the sentence of death had been carried out by the state of Florida. The people of the state of Florida. Weren't the people of the state already present in the execution? If someone says that they support capital punishment, then they had better be willing to sit right there in the chamber and watch it being carried out, because it's being done for them. The people of the state. The supporters of the death penalty. They have an obligation to take part in the killing. If they can't do that, then they need to reconsider how much they support the idea of executing someone.

But I didn't tell all that to the woman waiting for her fried fish platter. She and the employees of the restaurant continued to hurl questions at me for about ten more minutes. I didn't enjoy the interrogation, but in an odd way I began to feel better as I explained to them what happened. After all, I kept telling myself, that's why I did it. To explain to others what happens in a death chamber. I saw it and I was going to help others make sense of something that didn't make sense to me.

CHAPTER TWENTY-THREE

With my hunger satiated by the platter of disgusting, fried seafood, I drove my rental car back to the hotel. As I made my way from the parking lot to my room, I passed the Denny's restaurant where earlier that day I had seen Robert Ruger's family. It seemed like years ago.

I shifted the Wal-Mart bag I carried and unlocked the door to my room. Once inside, I checked all the usual places for any killers who might be waiting for me. I found that there were none. I knew I had to call my wife, but I didn't know what to say or how to say it. Camille was right. I couldn't handle it. I could not handle what I had just seen, and I felt unworthy to talk with her. I would forever be the dark stain in her life. She could cover it up and ignore it, but it could never be cleaned.

Trembling, I sat on the filthy bedspread staring at the phone. I had read somewhere that motels seldom wash the bedspreads in the rooms, only the sheets and pillowcases. I thought of this as I lowered my face to rest on the slick, satiny fabric. I smelled the sweat, and body fluids, of dozens of strangers who had found passion and peace in that room. I hated myself but was far too afraid to die.

I couldn't call her.

The phone was in my hand and Camille's voice on the line. I lied to her. I didn't like doing it, but I lied to her. I lied with every poisoned cell in my stricken body. "I'm fine," I told her. "Really. It was hard, but I did it. So how are the boys? Good. Do they miss me? Really? What did they do today? Oh, how cute. No, really, I'm fine. Maybe I shouldn't be fine, but interestingly, Camille, I am doing OK I'm actually very tired. Yeah, I know. It is probably psychological, but nonetheless, I'm dead tired, sorry, you know what I mean. I don't mean that I'm 'dead tired,' I mean I'm just exhausted. OK, I will. I'm going to visit the university library in Gainesville tomorrow so I probably won't talk to you until tomorrow night. No, I'm fine. Thanks, I will pray for you, too. Sleep well. Seriously, I'm fine. Maybe I shouldn't be, but it really wasn't that big of a deal. I'm fine, OK? All right, I'll talk to you tomorrow. Goodnight, I love you."

I hung up the phone and hated myself for lying to her. I was not fine, but I didn't want to worry or hurt her. I didn't want her to know that her husband was ripping himself apart in a dirty motel room in Florida.

I turned on every light in the room.

I sat and stared at the television. It was turned off and it looked very empty.

I wanted to feel better. I wanted morphine or some other kind of narcotic. During my first two years of college I used drugs regularly, but quit when I became a Christian in my early 20s. Right before my baptism, on my 21st birthday, I promised God that I would no longer use drugs. I hadn't overdosed, I hadn't been arrested, and I wasn't in trouble. I just thought that He would prefer that I not do that to myself anymore, and I gladly gave drugs up to be closer to Him.

But right then I was dying and I wanted something to pacify me. Had drugs been available to me that night, alone in that motel room, I might have taken them. I needed to warm the cold space inside me that had recently housed my self worth. Castro had been given Valium before his death and I wanted some Valium, too. I wondered if the prison counselor could have given me some Valium if she knew I was losing my mind? I should have talked to her.

I wanted to slip myself into nonexistence. I thought I might simply float away, like a bad idea. But I didn't want that. I needed peace of mind, not unconsciousness, and I needed it before I did something that I might not live to regret. I wanted to touch my children. I wanted to crawl into bed with them while they slept. I wanted to turn their mouths toward me and feel their warm breath on my face.

I wanted to touch something pure and spotless.

I wanted myself back.

I was dead, and I wanted so badly to be alive again.

I couldn't bring myself to cry, only to rub my face on the worn, used bedspread and imagine that I was not alone in that room. I imagined that I was with the countless people whose filth and sweat I could smell on the fabric ...

I knelt by that impure altar and prayed. I begged forgiveness, but I was unsure of what I had done wrong. I was guilty but I didn't know exactly what I was guilty of. I was sure that my punishment loomed over me, waiting to crush the fragile life out of me.

I prayed more, and then I felt guilty for being so near God's purity and goodness. On my unworthy, knees I cried and begged for peace, but all I could think of was how I had just killed a man and how I was unworthy to approach the Lord. I asked for resolution and forgiveness but did not find it. I was dying, and I was going to do so alone. Jesus Christ is often referred to as the Comforter in the Scriptures, but I could not find comfort from Him that night. I had pushed myself away from him, like a baby bird that jumps out of the nest and finds that he can't yet fly on his own.

My mind moved in a cold and slow motion. I rose from my knees and lay on the bed, still dressed in the "professional attire" I had worn for the execution. I situated myself on my back, with my arms outstretched and my feet toward the headboard, and stared straight up at the ceiling. In a moment of sheer terror I recognized the crucifix position and when I had last seen it. Just hours before, Edward Castro was lying in precisely the same position, staring at his ceiling in the death chamber.

The skin on my neck and arms crawled as if countless biting ants covered it. I bristled instantly and roughly stumbled out of the bed and fell onto the floor trying to rip from my mind that image of myself being strapped to a gurney. Quickly, I got up, as images of the execution slammed into my vulnerable mind. My chewed-down fingernails violently scratched my neck and arms and I grunted and swore as I pulled the clothing off my now frantic body. In my mind, Edward Castro looked at me, smiling to himself at my rapid decent into insanity. I shivered and looked at my nearly naked body in the mirror before me. Sweat covered my face and I desperately needed a shower, but I was too afraid to be nude and vulnerable under the hot water.

I sat on the padded chair in the corner of the room and stared at the wall. A painting of a girl feeding ducks on a placid pond stared back at me. I wondered if the girl in the picture, in her white cotton dress and her blue hair ribbon, had ever witnessed a violent murder. I wondered if she had baked rat poison into the bread that she was now feeding the unsuspecting ducks. In a moment, the bread would be gone, and she would sit on the mossy ground and watch the poison take effect on the ducks.

The sweet-looking girl in the painting smiled slightly. Maybe she had once been gang-raped and the six men who raped her were all going to be executed later that day. Perhaps she had come down to the duck pond before the execution to feed the ducks and reflect on the sweetness of revenge.

What seemed like weeks passed as I sat in the chair, and eventually I turned on the television. I watched about five minutes of a war movie. The killing of bad guys was provided as a source of entertainment for us, the viewers. In the bit of the one scene I watched, a soldier had been shot and was now eloquently explaining the virtues of bravery to his friend before he died. I recalled an old poem, written by a soldier in World War I, ironically entitled "It Is Sweet and Becoming to Die for One's Country." I turned off the television and tried again to pray and find comfort or peace. This time I felt a little better than I had two hours before, when I had last tried asking for God's help.

Later, I went to sleep and dreamed of dying, Mexican children.

CHAPTER TWENTY-FOUR

The next day, I drove around Starke and Gainesville. The morning was bright but the day felt empty and pointless. Had Castro's execution been postponed and Ruger's carried out, I would have spent that Friday preparing to watch a different execution. As it turned out, there would be no executions that day in Florida, and I had already seen enough. I spent my second Florida day in solitary confusion.

To distract myself and pass the time, I caught a mid-day movie, "Proof of Life," starring Meg Ryan and Russell Crowe. As I bought the ticket, I briefly questioned my decision to see a movie with that title the day after watching someone being killed. But I had not yet seen a movie with the actor Russell Crowe, and I had to find out for myself why all of the women I knew were in love with him.

In the film, a guy gets kidnapped and his employer hires Crowe to find him and negotiate his ransom. Meg Ryan plays the wife of the kidnapped man, and she falls in love with Crowe while her husband spends month after month as a hostage. I wondered, if Crowe loved the man's wife, did he really want to find her husband?

But, to his credit, Crowe appeared to try in earnest to rescue the husband, despite the fact that if the guy was gone, he could have Meg Ryan to himself. I must admit that I got a little sick each time he killed a bad guy in the movie. Granted, I was impressed because I had only killed one person the day before and I had nearly lost my mind, while Russell Crowe can kill lots of guys and it didn't appear to adversely affect him in the least.

Trying to understand it objectively, I constantly wondered what it was about the execution that affected me so strongly. I had been trained in criminology and the social sciences. I knew what I was getting into, so why was I so surprised and shocked? My execution-friend, David, had told me the night before, as we stood in the parking lot, "You'll be OK, you're a smart guy." So why was I not feeling OK?

I was supposed to be the observer of an execution, not a participant. I wasn't supposed to feel this way, but I did. Why? What had I done wrong? Was it talking to Ruger's family? Did that make it too personal? Too real?

Or was I experiencing remorse of some kind? Before the execution, I had found, much to my embarrassment and guilt, that I was hoping that at least one of the scheduled executions would not be postponed because after traveling so far, it would be a disappointment not to see what I had specifically come to watch. Was that producing guilt in me? It was my job to understand these feelings I was having, but I couldn't.

I traveled to Florida with the image of myself as a professor, detached from the subject. I went as an educated man who studied human beings and what drives our behavior. Horrible images were not new to me. I had watched videos of suicides and studied countless diagrams and photos of murder scenes. In some of my classes I even show photos of victims, in an effort to help others understand what a killer does, and why he attacked the victim in a particular way. But this was different, and I knew it.

The death scenes I had previously viewed were just that ... scenes. Like a movie, they weren't real to me. And more importantly, they had nothing to do with me personally. This execution, however, was related to me. It was personal because I had helped do it. I helped to execute Edward Castro. No academic training, no theory, no intellectual approach could distance me from that fact.

I might have remained detached had I not gone inside the execution chamber. Had I only interviewed family members, guards, prison officials, and maybe a few psychologists, I would still have uncovered good information but I would have avoided actually participating in the execution myself. I would probably be fine right now, instead of a mess. If I hadn't signed my name to the form counting me as an Official Witness, I might have remained a detached researcher. Instead, I now felt like a killer.

But I did sign that form. Why? Why had I possessed such a strong need to understand executions first hand? What it feels like and how it affects people? I wanted to know what it was like, and now I do. It hurts. And the pain, anguish, and fear didn't seem to be getting better very quickly.

Only now, after the event, did I understand the difference between "watching" an execution and "witnessing" one. I had come to Florida to watch an execution, not realizing that I would actually witness it. The subtle distinction is important. When a person watches something, like a movie or a television show, he is not part of the episode. He is merely an observer. A witness, on the other hand, is a person involved with the outcome of the event. At a trial, witnesses testify as to what happened, but those simply watching from the courtroom do not take the stand. In professional sports, a fan buys a ticket to "watch" the game, not to "witness" it. He is not on the playing field with the team. Someone watching merely stands on the sidelines, not participating. But a witness is relevant, helping shape the outcome of the event.

I misunderstood. I had come to Florida to "watch" an execution, not recognizing that the state needed a "witness." The newspaper reporters in the back row of the chamber were the ones "watching" the execution. Because they observed Castro, the prison employees, and the witnesses and then reported their findings to their readers. However, I sat in the front row, next to the killer, and "witnessed" his execution.

I realized that I would never have been invited into the chamber if I had said in my letter to the State of Florida that I wanted to "watch" an execution. By chance, I had used the word "witness," and I used it twice in that fateful letter. I had asked to take part in the execution of another person, when I really thought I was asking to "see" it happen. I wanted to study it; I didn't want to become part of the study. But I had become a part of Edward Castro's execution, and now it was a part of me.

That afternoon, I drove around Gainesville looking at everything, but not concentrating on much of anything at all. I spotted a bookstore, one of the large chains, and knew I had to go in. Bookstores often serve as a sanctuary for me. There I could sit in the comfortable chairs for as long as I wanted, reading whatever looked interesting at the time, but never having to buy a thing.

Probably out of habit, I approached the crime section of the store and picked up a paperback book on Andrew Cunanan. He was the man who murdered fashion designer Gianni Versace, right here in Florida. Flipping through the pages, I came upon the photo section in the middle of the book. There I saw a photo of Cunanan, sitting upright on a bed, with blood coming out of his mouth, nose and ears. He had just shot himself in the head.

I began to suspect that death was waiting for me everywhere I went. Nausea rippled through my stomach and my hands started to slightly tremble. I closed the book and put it back on the shelf. I didn't want to ever see death or think about killers again. I hated the image of the gunshot victim I had just seen, and I thought, for the hundredth time that day, that I had killed a man and would be forced to live with that guilt for whatever was left of my life.

I contemplated different ways to end the guilt, grief and pain that I had brought upon myself. Looking for something more innocuous to read, I went to the children's section and browsed the shelves. There I spotted the book, *Good Night Moon*. I was familiar with the story, since it was written for toddlers and I had three of them. I sat down to lose myself in the innocence of the story.

Good Night Moon is a picture book by Margaret Wice Brown about a little bunny. In his big, green bedroom, the bunny says good night to everything in the room before he goes to sleep. While the author didn't say this, I suspected that the bunny was stalling because he didn't want to go to sleep. He says goodnight to everything in the room, including the air, before he is ready for bed. I understood his tactic. Why would he want to simply end it all when there is still so much to see and so much to do? Dylan Thomas, in his famous poem, told his dad, "do not go gently into that goodnight," and Robert Frost said he, too, "had miles to go before I sleep." Why would the little bunny want to rush off to sleep without saying goodnight to everything he sees, stalling his ending as long as possible.

Thinking of this, I left the bookstore, drove back to Starke, parked my car in the hotel parking lot, and went back up to my room. I opened the door, stepped inside the room, and closed the door. It didn't seem important to check and see, as I always do, if there were any psychotic killers hiding in there. I closed the curtain and stood in the cool room with the lights turned off. A sliver of sunlight found its way through the crack in the curtains and rested itself on the bed.

I had killed a man, and I was contemplating sleep.

Like Dylan Thomas' dad.

Like Robert Frost thought about when his woods filled up with snow.

I wasn't exactly tired of everything, but with the guilt, I didn't know if I wanted to keep my eyes open any longer. It would be relaxing to strip down and lie between the cool sheets as I drifted off. It would feel like floating on a satiny cloud and my body might be warmer where the sharp slice of sunlight was heating the comforter, spilling off the bed and dripping in a red pool onto the floor.

I stood near the doorway in the motel room scratching my wrists and looking at the bed, wondering if it would make everything better. If I did it, would I have torturous dreams where I am struggling but can't find comfort or peace? That certainly wouldn't feel like the resolution I was seeking. If I cried out while drifting off, no one would be there to stop me and tell me everything would be fine. I was all alone and sleep was inviting. In my mind, I recited what I remembered the bunny in *Good Night Moon* had said,

> "Goodnight moon.
> Goodnight stars.
> Goodnight air.
> Goodnight nobody.
> But ..."

I thought of my kids, and my wife.

I decided that I would turn in later, much later. I had too many things left to do, and miles to go before I slept.

I left the motel room, got back into the rental car, and drove toward the prison to see how it looked in the daylight.

CHAPTER TWENTY-FIVE

Driving to the prison, for the second time in 24 hours, I thought about the other 11 witnesses and wondered what they were doing right at that moment. I imagined that most of them were at work. Even those that were retired were probably doing whatever they had done the day before the execution. Everyone else was getting on with his life. Everyone, except me.

In the van the night before, after the execution was over, I had stared at the other witnesses to see how they were holding up. At the time, I didn't notice much, other than that we were all acting guilty and detached from each other. It had been a strange reaction, since people in a group generally bond together after a traumatic event. As members of this extraordinarily unique group, we should all have hugged one another and asked, "Are you all right? Are you sure you're OK?"

But we didn't do that. Nobody talked to their fellow witness, let alone hugged him. There were no questions about the emotional state of the others. We didn't even look at each other. In short, we behaved like individuals rather than a group.

Groups arise when people share some common interest or common view of the world. There are countless groups and most of us are members of several of them at the same time. We are members of groups of students, groups of friends at work, groups of single parents, church groups, neighborhood groups, and so on. In each case there is some common element that holds us together.

Thus, a gathering of random people in a McDonalds restaurant at noon isn't really a group. They rarely interact or talk to one another at all. There just isn't a reason to. These patrons don't have a common identity, they just happen to be eating lunch in the same place at the same time. Most people don't consider the simple act of eating at a McDonalds a significant part of their identity as a person.

However, parents of little kids playing together in the jungle-gym area of that same McDonalds will often strike up conversations with each other. Unlike eating lunch at a fast-food restaurant, children are often an important part of one's identity. While the kids play, the adults sit with each other and talk, not surprisingly, almost exclusively about their kids. They become a group, even if they didn't know each other before that day. So why were the 12 people who witnessed the Castro execution not a group? We interacted with each other a great deal before the execution, as we all waiting for this enormously important event. But afterwards, we didn't interact at all. Instead, we acted like strangers who happened to be in the same place at the same time, just like most of the people do in a McDonalds.

As I drove back toward the Florida State Prison that late afternoon, I began to understand why the 12 of us did not behave like a group after the execution. We didn't act as though we shared a common identity because we didn't. It was complicated, but I wondered if it might be because each of us witnessed the event for a different reason.

I traveled to Starke in an effort to better understand what an execution was like. I wanted to see for myself exactly what happens behind the closed doors, and how the events affected the different people involved. I came to study the whole process.

David, on the other hand, was there for vengeance. He had seen so much violence and carnage that he needed to see justice done. I believed that David used executions as a way to reassure himself that a high price had been paid for all the trauma he had seen.

Lewis, the grandfatherly witness whose leg I rested mine against, was a retired police officer. Perhaps he needed to feel that he was still part of the crime-fighting process on the streets in his community. He was past the point in his career of apprehending criminals, but he could still be involved in seeing that justice was carried out.

Bill, the retired narcotics officer with the long ponytail, came to the prison that day because, as he pointed out, killers were evil. He watched the execution the same way a kid might watch an action movie. He rooted for the hero, who almost always represents good and, in the movies, good always triumphs over evil. I imagined that Bill's attendance at the execution was something like rooting for the good guys to defeat evil. He might have been the only one feeling happy or victorious at the end of the execution, since he went into the death chamber hoping to see the "bad guy" lose the game. And Castro did lose.

While I didn't talk as much with the other eight witnesses, I suspected that each one had his or her own reasons for attending the execution. The decision that motivated each one of us to take the seat in the death chamber was a highly personal one. After it was over, we each realized in our own way that we weren't a close group. Instead, we were actually a collection of individuals with our own emotional baggage, our own reasons for taking part in the killing, and our own unique view of what had just happened.

I was reminded of the 1957 film "Twelve Angry Men," starring Henry Fonda, which was later remade with Jack Lemmon. In the picture, 12 jurors in a trial find that they each have personal, and certainly not objective, reasons for reaching the verdict they did in a trial. Like these jurors, the various motivations of the witnesses at Castro's execution ultimately determined how each one would feel about it after it was over.

I thought of this as I drove out toward the prison. During the drive, I passed a magnificent white and blue church that I remembered seeing on the drive to the prison the previous afternoon. The elongated structure and pitched roof looked like a great bird in flight. I pulled off the side of the road and took out my camera, the same one that the officer with the clipboard nearly confiscated the day before. I took a couple of pictures of the building, which was situated about 150 yards away from the road.

I noticed that one of the handful of vehicles in the church parking lot nearest to me, an old red pickup truck, was now driving directly toward me. I panicked and quickly got back into my car, pulling out onto the road and toward the prison. The truck gained speed on me as I drove away and as I approached the same "prisons in the area" sign I recognized from the day before, it pulled up directly behind me. At first I thought I might be acting paranoid and that I wasn't really being chased. But then the truck began flashing its lights at me, and the driver stuck his hand out the window and waved his hand at me to pull over.

Maybe I shouldn't have taken pictures of the church. I probably offended someone and now I was going to get beaten up on the side of the road near the prison in Starke, Florida. I couldn't help but wonder, "What is the deal with cameras and people in Florida?"

My heart was beating hard and I was breathing heavily as I thought about my escape plan. I pulled off to the side of the road, where I intended to wait just long enough for the driver to get out of his truck. Then I would speed off, turning back toward town, and try to lose him as he was standing outside his vehicle. If I used side roads, I might reach town before he caught up with me.

I looked in my rearview mirror and waited for the two attackers to get out of their truck behind me. I noticed that the man and woman walking toward my car from the truck were both about 70 years old. Maybe I could defend myself after all.

Cautiously, I got out of my car, and as I did, I heard the man say, "Yeah, I thought that was you. How are you doing?" I didn't recognize his smiling face, but not wanting to sound rude, I answered politely, "Oh, I'm well. How are you two doing?"

They both smiled and he said, "We can't complain. It's such a pretty day today, and all." The man then said to the woman with him, "Dear, this here is Dr. Diaz, the young fellow from the university I told you about last night."

The kind smile on his face suddenly registered with me, and I remembered that this was Lewis, the grandfatherly man I had sat next to in the death chamber the night before. He explained that he was a parishioner at the church I had just photographed. As he and his wife were leaving the church parking lot, he saw me and wanted to introduce me to his wife.

"Your church is elegant. It impressed me so much that I wanted to take a photo of it," I told him.

Lewis looked pleased and he replied, "Thank you," in a tone that sounded very sincere.

We now had something in common: our mutual interest in his church. Lewis and I began to talk easily. The night before, we were both witnesses at an execution for different reasons. When it was over we had nothing to say to each other. But the day after, admiring the beauty of his place of worship, we spoke as friends and I felt quite relaxed around him.

"So how are you doing?" Lewis wanted to know. He really did sound concerned.

"I'm still very confused and scared about it," I confided in him and his wife. "I really don't know what to think about what I just saw."

With a puzzled expression, Lewis then asked, "What do you mean 'what you just saw?' Are you talking about the execution?"

"Yeah, of course that's what I'm talking about. I feel sick about it, and I guess I just don't think it was the right thing to do."

Lewis glanced at his wife, who hadn't said much of anything since we started talking. He looked uncomfortable, and perhaps a little embarrassed for me. "Are you a Christian, Joseph?" he asked me.

"Yes, sir, I am."

"Well," he continued, "after watching a few executions, in the electric chair and by lethal injection, I know that executions are the right thing to do. It's really the only Christian thing to do to killers."

I didn't know how to respond. I was shocked. This gentle old man, who reminded me of my grandpa, believed that the horrible spectacle I had seen the night before was part of the same religious faith that I held dear to me. I had no counter to an argument like that. Lewis not only believed that executions were compatible with being Christian; he also thought they were necessary to Christianity.

I didn't think there was much of a chance that I would change his mind, so I left it at that. Besides, I didn't want to argue with him. We would both continue to embrace our religious faith, he in his way, and me in mine. But on this issue, an issue as serious as life and death, we couldn't agree. And yet we would both go forward considering ourselves to be followers of Jesus Christ.

We meekly smiled at our impasse, and awkwardly looked for a phrase that would signal our separation. I tried, "Well, I think I will drive out to the prison and see what it looks like on days when there's no execution."

Lewis replied, "Yep, we're gonna go on home and see what's what." See what's what. I always loved that line. See what's what.

I asked Lewis' wife to take a picture of him and me together. We stood by the large, red sign that announced there were prisons in the area. Then we shook hands, like old friends, and began to go on with our day. I wished them both a good day, and they told me to have a safe trip back to Minnesota.

As they walked away, Lewis' wife, whose name I was never told, turned and said, "We're gonna be going through Minnesota next summer." Reminded of that fact, Lewis turned around quickly and said, "That's right. What town are you in? We could stop by and say 'hello' and meet your family."

"You bet!" I said, smiling at them both. "If you're in the area, please stop by and say hello."

They both beamed back at me, as though this was a grand idea. Then they turned and got back into their truck. Lewis and his wife drove off without ever asking for my address or telephone number. I didn't expect to see them next summer.

I drove the rental car the last mile or so to the prison and found that it looked very much like it had the day before. The only difference I could discern was that no cars lined the roads, and no police officers gathered at the entrance. The parking lot looked nearly empty, too. Without the impending execution, things were much quieter.

I decided to keep going toward the prison. I guess I just wanted to see what the Florida State Prison looked like up close, when my mind wasn't preoccupied with a pending execution. But I didn't really have a reason to go in. I certainly hadn't dressed "professionally," wearing sweat pants instead, so I couldn't claim to have a meeting with the warden.

Much to my surprise, the gate was actually completely unattended. The road only led to the parking lot, which sat outside the prison fence, so there was no way I could grab a prisoner or two and throw them in my trunk. But the day before, police officers carefully screened everyone who even wanted to park near the prison. Today there was, literally, no one guarding the front entryway to the prison and I drove right through the open entry.

After about a 100 yards the road divided. To the left it led to the employee parking lot and the red brick building where I had gone the night before. I glanced down the road to the right and my heart rate immediately picked up. Now that it was daylight, and I was more familiar with the prison grounds, I could see the death house.

I followed the road to the right and entered a parking area just large enough to hold two or three cars. The lot sat adjacent to the monstrous fence that had intimidated me the day before. A tall, circular tower stood roughly 75 yards to the left of my parked car. I knew that it housed armed guards on continuous look out for escaped prisoners. The windows at the top of the tower were darkly tinted, but in the afternoon sun I could see the shapes of individuals moving around inside. It was also a very good bet that they could see me.

With my camera in my hand, I turned away from the tower and quickly walked the 15 feet toward the barbed wire. Only about 20 yards in front of me, on the other side of the fence, stood the death house for the state of Florida. It seemed unreal to me that just the evening before, I stood on the other side of that fence, with a group of 11 strangers, waiting for the execution of a serial killer.

I looked at the one door going into the building and remembered hearing my name being called, signing the unknown form, and walking through the door into the building. Unless you had been inside, you would never have known that the squat, little green structure with the numerous ventilation fans in the roof, had seen the killings of dozens and dozens of murderers. It was so small and nondescript that no passer-by would ever give it a second look.

I raised my camera, adjusted the zoom lens, and snapped off five pictures of the death house. I looked up again toward the guard tower and saw the outline of the guards who watched me. Nervously, I turned and quickly walked back to my car, then pulled out of the parking lot and headed back toward the unmanned gate.

Off to my right, from the direction of the warden's office, I spotted a pick-up truck with shield emblems on its doors driving toward me. The truck drove after my car as I passed the fork in the road. I was certain that I was going to get in trouble and this time I would probably lose the cheap camera that kept creating problems for me.

As my heart raced, I considered my options. I could take out the film, hide it under the seat, and put in a new roll, just in case the prison officials, who were now clearly chasing me, confiscated my film. But what if photographing the death house was illegal? In that case, it wouldn't be right for me to keep the film. More importantly, if I hid the film under the seat and they found it, I might be subjected to a more thorough search, including body cavities. I decided not to hide the film.

I cleared the gate and was just about to turn onto the highway and toward the relative safety of my motel room, when the truck began flashing its lights at me. I caught my breath and pulled off to the side of the highway in front of the prison. In my car, I waited to see how much trouble I was in, but the two men in the truck didn't get out. Instead, the driver stuck his hand out of the window and motioned for me to come back to his truck.

Leaving my camera on the seat, I stepped outside and cautiously walked back toward them. I approached the driver's window and saw that inside the cab of the truck, with the seal of the State of Florida emblazoned on the door, were a prison guard and an inmate. The guard looked serious, but the prisoner had a big smile on his face and did not try to hide the fact that he was laughing at me.

I noticed that the guard didn't carry a gun and the prisoner wasn't handcuffed. Since Starke boasted the most maximum of all the maximum-security prisons, I wondered what the prisoner had done to get sent here. Then I wondered how the guard could feel safe around him, because I sure didn't.

Without giving the man a chance to speak first, I quickly explained, "Hi, I'm Dr. Joseph Diaz. I'm a criminologist from Minnesota and I was down here yesterday for the Castro execution." The guard looked at me skeptically, but he didn't say anything. I continued, "I was told yesterday, by some officer at the front gate, that there are no pictures allowed on execution days. So I came back today to take a few pictures of the prison."

I was nervous, so the likelihood of me shutting up anytime soon was pretty low. I continued, "Am I not supposed to take pictures of the prison ever?"

The prisoner grinned even more, and actually started to giggle. I seldom hear grown men giggle, and have never heard a maximum-security prisoner do this, but he was obviously enjoying himself at my expense. The guard finally spoke and said, "So you're a criminologist?"

"Yes," I confirmed quickly, glad that he had heard at least some of what I had said. "I'm a professor of criminology and sociology at a university in Minnesota. I just wanted some pictures and now I'm done, so can I go?"

The prisoner started giggling again, and then licked his lips. Meanwhile, the guard stared into space, carefully considering my request. The guard looked over toward the prisoner, away from me, and nodded his head to no one. The prisoner didn't notice the guard looking toward him because he was openly staring at me and softly chuckling to himself. I began to suspect the two men had been smoking something right before they were sent over to see what I was up to, and the giggles and glazed looks that they both had in abundance were the result of being stoned.

Finally, the driver of the truck came to a decision, and he announced it with an air of importance, "Well … I guess you can keep your camera and the pictures. But don't take any more pictures of the prison. I could take your camera away and you wouldn't get it back." I got the feeling he just didn't want to bother with me. He decided to simply let me go so he and the prisoner could go back to doing whatever they were doing moments before. That was fine with me, and I returned to my car.

I was relieved to get back to the motel. After unlocking the door, I once again checked the room for sociopathic serial killers. Having found none, I dialed my home telephone number. Camille and I chatted for a while, about nothing in particular, before I lay down on the bed and turned on the television. Around 9:00 that evening, after watching some pointless action movie in which Lorenzo Lamas had to shoot and kill lots of bad guys, I forced myself to attempt sleep.

CHAPTER TWENTY-SIX

I was up early the next morning, and on my way to the airport. I was anxious to get home; back to Minnesota, to Camille, and to my kids. While my stay in Florida lasted less than 48 hours, it seemed like an eternity had passed since I shared the rental car shuttle bus with the Jacksonville Jaguars guy.

The United States presidential election was still in dispute and Florida would decide its outcome. Did Al Gore win or would the election go to George Bush? It seemed like the attention of the entire world was focused on that state.

Everyone I stood in line with that Saturday morning at the airport had some opinion on the matter. One lady rationalized, "If he got more votes, he won," while I overheard someone else claim, " ... but it's unconstitutional!" Still another traveler tried to explain, "That's what the Electoral College is for, cases just like this. I mean just like this!"

They had all become experts on the American electoral process, and most of them near me seemed to believe that George W. would ultimately prevail and become the next President. Although I had voted a month before, I now didn't care who won the election. It just didn't seem to matter anymore.

"Where are you headed today, sir?" It was my turn at the counter and I approached the smiling ticket agent.

"Minneapolis," I replied, as I handed her my ticket and identification. She verified that I was who I said I was, and began typing into her computer.

"Did you enjoy your stay in the Jacksonville area?" Her question startled me and I was not in the mood to expend energy trying to think of something socially acceptable to say.

"Not really," I told her truthfully. "It was not at all what I expected."

To her credit, the ticket agent looked genuinely saddened and concerned. "Oh, I'm sorry," she gushed. "Were you here on business or pleasure?"

"Neither really," I explained, "it was a research trip."

I thought that might satisfy her and end the conversation that I didn't want to have, but she pressed on, "What type of research do you do?"

"I do research into violent criminal behavior," I told her. I didn't want to do this so early in the morning, to her or to me, but I continued anyway, "I was in the area watching a man named Edward Castro, a serial killer, be executed on Thursday."

She must hear that type of comment regularly from her customers because other than casually glancing up at me, she didn't appear at all surprised. "Wasn't that hard?" she asked in a conversational tone. "I mean, I don't know if I could do that. I'm in favor of the death penalty and everything, but I couldn't do that," she added matter-of-factly.

I noticed that she was wearing a gold cross on a chain around her neck, proclaiming her Christian faith. Her statement confused me and I asked, "You couldn't do what? Watch an execution?"

"Exactly. I couldn't do it. I couldn't watch it. I think we should have them and all, but I could never watch one myself. I just couldn't handle being in there and seeing something like that." This reminded me of the other customer I had encountered at the fried fish joint on Thursday evening. That woman "supported" executions, but didn't think she could watch one either.

I couldn't let this one go unchallenged. "Don't you think that if an execution is too hard for you to watch, maybe you should re-consider whether or not you support it?" I asked her. "I mean, yes, they are horrible and disgusting, which is why I am now opposed to them. I could never watch one again. But if you support capital punishment, don't you think you had better be willing to sit right in there and watch someone die? You can't have it both ways. You can't support something and not be willing to do it yourself. If you support executions, you had better be willing to sit in there and watch criminals being killed. Further, if you were asked to, you had better be willing to throw the switch, or pull the trigger, or give that lethal injection. If you can't do that, if you can't physically kill them yourself, then you had better not say you support the death penalty because you obviously have some reservations about the whole process."

The ticket agent looked a little panicked as she stared at her computer screen, typing and acting like she hadn't heard me. She didn't pursue the conversation any further and without looking at me, gave me my ticket, directed me to the gate and told me to have a nice flight. I'm sure that after I left, she probably rolled her eyes and told her coworkers, "Geez, what a weirdo!" But I hoped she at least thought about what I said.

Throughout the concourse, I passed families walking together toward their destinations. Some looked happy and excited, just arriving in the sunshine state. Others, those of us heading home, were worn out and tired. With my ticket in hand, I sat at the gate, waiting to return to Minnesota. I didn't know what I would find there, or what my family would find in me, but I knew that I was a different man.

By my feet sat a little boy, perhaps a year old. He sat on the floor examining a set of car keys as his mother looked on. The young child decided that the keys looked edible, and he began to chew on them. His mother smiled with pride at the innocence that sat before her on the dirty and stained carpeting.

I watched the baby and he eventually looked up at me. We stared at each other for a few moments so he took the keys out of his mouth and proudly showed them to me. I smiled at him to reward his accomplishment. I thought how all of us started out our lives as innocent as that little boy. But then, sadly, some of us turn, or are turned by others, into dangerous monsters.

After a short wait, my flight was called and I boarded the plane. I found the correct seat and buckled myself into it. I turned on the vent, closed my eyes, and waited for my self-induced coma to wash over me before take-off. Like always, I was sure the plane was going to crash and I was going to be killed. However, much to my surprise, I wasn't exactly afraid of that happening anymore. I thought that I still might die in an airplane, but, interestingly, it no longer scared me.

The corners of my mouth turned up into a smile as I thought of my small victory over the fear of death.

I would not, however, open my eyes.

My death might come, but I was not going to watch it again.

THE END

AUTHOR BIOGRAPHY

Dr. Joseph D. Diaz was born in 1971 in Joliet, Illinois. He earned a Bachelor's Degree in 1995 from Utah State University, a Master's Degree in 1997 from the University of Nevada Las Vegas, and a Ph.D. in 1999 from University of Nevada Las Vegas. He is a Professor of Sociology at Southwest State University in Marshall, Minnesota and concentrates his teaching and research in the area of criminology and antisocial behavior.

Dr. Diaz has written studies on suicide, community violence, poverty, religion, gambling, and social problems, and racism in communities. He is often a featured speaker at conferences, workshops and schools where he discusses crime, suicide, gangs, drugs, racism and ways that communities and individuals can combat these social problems. He has been featured on diverse news programs ranging from regional radio and television stations to the Discovery Channel and Canadian Public Radio.

Dr. Diaz lives with his wife Camille and his young children in a blue house, that used to be pink, with lots of flowers in Marshall, Minnesota. His e-mail address is drjosephdiaz@ponchapress.com.

Portrait by Steve Allen

AUTHOR, JOSEPH D. DIAZ, PH.D.

ABOUT PONCHA PRESS

Poncha Press strives to recognize new voices in the writing community, and to publish quality nonfiction and fiction works in wide range of genres. Our mission is to identify talented, interesting, and previously unpublished writers and make their work available to readers.

Poncha Press donates a portion of its annual profits to U.S. charities dedicated to improving the welfare of animals. The company is located in Morrison, Colorado, in the foothills of the Rocky Mountains. To order books, or for more information about Poncha Press, please visit our Web site at www.ponchapress.com or call us, toll-free, at 1-888-350-1445.